Notes on Participatory Art

Toward a manifesto differentiating it from Open Work, Interactive Art and Relational Art.

Gustaf Almenberg

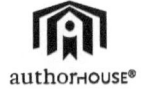

authorHOUSE®

AuthorHouse™ UK Ltd.
500 Avebury Boulevard
Central Milton Keynes, MK9 2BE
www.authorhouse.co.uk
Phone: 08001974150

First published by AuthorHouse 11/2/2010

ISBN: 978-1-4520-9928-6

This book is printed on acid-free paper.

To those Avant Garde artists mentioned in this book, who made the effort to communicate with us not only through their art, but also through their writings.

Contents

My ambition is to fuse a world-
view with a pure making of art.
Paul Klee, Bauhaus 1924[1]

Introduction

Quite in line with the subject matter of this book, this is
very much a work in progress. Thus I have chosen to call
it Notes and also to emphasize that I hope that this is just
a beginning and that more information and reactions
will flow in from the readers. I do not claim to cover the
whole field, in terms of time, geography and scope, of the
topic I am beginning to map out. Nor is it an exhaustive
list of all artists who has ever made a work of art in the
vein of Participatory Art.

Thanks to the new POD technology, new editions of this
book will hopefully come out fairly soon as more material
comes in. If you have any suggestions for additions or
changes in this text I will be happy to receive them in an
email to: gustaf@almenberg.com.

Why does one write a book like this one? As an artist you
certainly don't have to build a theory out of your own
art. Art speaks for itself some people would claim, and
does not – indeed should not – need any explanations.
This may be true to some extent. There are exceptions,
however. Art that is not mainstream for one reason or
other may need some kind of verbal introduction in order
to be perceived. Art that is at the periphery of its time,
either for reasons of geography or commercial interest or

because it is simply different in its historical context, may well disappear unnoticed if it were not for the support of the written word. It might be worth remembering that art history like all history is written by the survivors...

Few but at least some artists who later – often much later – won great acclaim have been "writing artists." Piet Mondrian is a prime example, but also Paul Klee and Vassily Kandinsky, among other early modernists. As an artist I have written this in order to understand consciously what I am doing subconsciously in my art. This book contains my notes made as I was trying to find the predecessors to my thinking and my praxis, trying to find out if there was a tradition that I belonged to. Had others been searching along the same path I had and if so, what had they found? By publishing these notes I hope to stimulate others searching along the same path to continue doing so and get in touch, to perhaps find common ground.

Another reason to write this book is to rescue from oblivion some interesting thoughts and ideas that have fallen outside the immediate interest of the contemporary discussion among those interested in art who are non-specialists. A prime example came to my attention as I had almost finished writing. For reasons I don't remember I came across Umberto Eco's in my view highly important book *The Open Work* only toward the end of writing this book. How come I almost missed it? Well, nearly half a century had passed since Eco wrote his book and it was no longer promoted by any commercial interests; and finding it on the Internet required that you were familiar with the key concept "open work" and its meaning. Art discourse is focusing on different issues today. If for no other reason I believe this book serves the purpose of rescuing to our times the highly interesting and creative thoughts of some of the crucial artists of the avant-garde in Modernism.

Why then a manifesto and what gives me the right to propose a manifesto for Participatory Art? Manifestos have a long tradition in art and within the Modern Movement in particular. Manifestos serve as a kind of rallying point for people with similar ideas in order for them to encourage each other in their work and to develop these ideas further. Personally I used the term Participatory Art at my first solo exhibition in Stockholm, Sweden in 1982. To my knowledge no one else had used this term up till then. My inspiration at that time came from the concept Participatory Democracy that I had come across about 15 years earlier.

PART I

TOWARD A MANIFESTO OF PARTICIPATORY ART

If it is true that every age is reflected in its own art, as claimed by artists like Piet Mondrian, Lazlo Moholy-Nagy and others at the beginning of Modernism, where then does art reflect the age we are entering now in the early 21st century? Might perhaps our own age be described as the Age of Participation? If this description fits best, which art then best represents this age? Does this art even exist today? Or, has it existed for quite some time already, but, like most pioneering work, it has simply not been noticed, because, being ahead of its time, it has not reflected contemporary times and hence went unrecognized?

The kind of art that I view as most emblematic of our age, is what I call Participatory Art. In the early 1980s, no one had heard of Participatory Art, and it is little known even today. Yet, I think this art reflects our own times better than any other kind of art.

"Welcome to the Participation Age!"

"Welcome to the Participation Age" wrote Scott Mc-Nealy in an article published in the Financial Times in June 2005[2]. McNealy was at that time chairman and

CEO of Sun Microsystems – an Information Technology company with over 31,000 employees in more than 100 countries. No doubt, McNealy was referring to the new cultural phenomenon of customer participation in product development and even product content.

McNealy elaborated on his statement by adding that this welcome "is based on the simple but powerful truths that innovation can happen anywhere, and the creating of connections and networks (through the new Internet) has a multiplier effect on *creativity*" (my italics).

Half a year later, "*Participation is the latest watchword*" was the headline of an article by Steve Prentice, vice-president and chief of Research at Gartner, the world's largest Information Technology research and advisory company.[3] The article referred to new Internet systems, sometimes called Web 2.0, powered by new technologies – Wiki, Ajax, Open Source Programming, all eventually leading to applications like E-bay, Wikipedia, MySpace, YouTube, Facebook etc. The Web 2.0 system has been described as an "*architecture of participation*" by Tim O'Reilly, a computer book publisher.[4]

This Participation Age is characterized and driven by the increasing trend in business to become customer-focused to the point where companies actually collaborate with customers in the making of the final product. Harvesting customer insights is fast becoming a crucial competence for many companies. Participation is fundamentally changing the way business is done and is clearly visible in mass media, politics and healthcare.[5] To the experts, another prime example is the open-source collaboration in the development of the web browser Firefox by

Mozilla. Firefox has about 150 million users all over the world. Approximately 40% of the code that created the program for Firefox did not come from employees but from self-selected volunteers[6].

The Participation age differs from preceding ages – and I am here talking about differences between ages, not between kinds of art – in that the Participation Age emanates at a time when industrial sector of the economy is rapidly shrinking, just like agriculture had shrunk at an earlier time. The industrial economy is replaced by the service economy or, perhaps, by now we should call it the experience economy. The organization of excellent production is no longer in focus but a given. The focus is now on the consumer and how to offer her or him a better consumer experience. Consumers are looking out not only for products but also from the experiences that come with the product, hence the steadily growing importance of brands and of the entertainment and leisure sectors in the economy.

English writer and artist John Ruskin of the 19th century epitomized the fear that human beings would be destroyed by industrialism, through the deadness of industrial people. Sociologist and philosopher Theodor W. Adorno voiced the fears of the 20th century that society would be destroyed by individuals being alienated from them selves. Neither could have foreseen a society where the consumer would be king, in choosing products and services, and also as a potential partner of corporations in everything from product development to product content. We are now entering an age where what defines you is what you choose to buy and not to buy, and maybe even more what you choose to participate in and not participate in. Perhaps it is no coincidence that fewer and fewer people wish to take part in ordinary politics, whereas more and more people seem to participate in action groups of various kinds.

Art in the Participation Age

Every age has its own art. "Art crystallizes the emotions of an age; art is mirror and voice", wrote Lazlo Moholy-Nagy.[7] He echoed Piet Mondrian's statement of 1917: "If art is to be a living reality for modern man, it has to be a pure expression of the new consciousness of the age."[8] Henri van de Velde, a leading figure in the Art Noveau movement, expressed a similar sentiment: "Art is changing its shape, because society is changing its shape."[9] Later, in 1931, Mondrian phrased it more to the point when he wrote that "the expression of art follows life, not nature."[10] As far back as in 1876, Stéphane Mallarmé saw the impressionists as connected to the advent of democracy.[11] After all, I believe a changing society was a strong driving force that made Dadaism and Symbolism replace Cubism as the dominant style after WW I; and a driving force behind abstract art in various forms such as American Expressionism just after WW II.

During most of the 20th century, the typical quest for art was simplicity and the very basics of human existence. My guess for the future, however, is that the quest for art during the Participation Age will be the productive participation of the many and hence of creativity as such.[12] It will also be a form of art that reflects the changing roles between producers and consumers; and therefore also an art that highlights the importance of individual choice.

In the Participation Age I believe the future belongs to those who can understand and enhance creativity and the conditions for creativity, as well as those who can *organize the creativity of the many* and *channel the creativity of the many into a cooperative and productive use.*

If it is true that we are now entering the Participation Age - an age of mass creativity - how then is this reflected in art? Would it not be in an art very much centered around precisely creativity and participation as such? But how come that art, which after all so often prides itself of being avant-garde, has not been in the vanguard of the Participation Age? Or has it? But we just haven't noticed it?

The spectator in a new role

To art critic Michael Fried reading Robert Morris it was clear that to Morris "The object, not the beholder, must remain the center or focus of the situation; but the situation itself *belongs to* the beholder."[13] In Participatory Art, neither the object nor the beholder is the focus of the situation. Rather, the focus is the very *act of creating*. Participatory Art is "the beholder in action" using personal choice and intuition as primary tools. This can be seen as parallel to the psychoanalyst D.W.Winnicott's "discovery" in the 1950s of a third kind of reality, that is neither the inner nor the outer reality postulated by traditional psychoanalysis, but a third or intermediate reality. Winnicott called this *play* and included it within the wider context of culture and art.[14]

In a 1997 essay on *site specific art*, Miwon Kwon claims that Minimalism can be seen as *giving the spectator a physical body.*[15] Kwon points out that this kind of art puts emphasis on the spectator immersing her/himself into the total experience of the site specific piece of art that encompasses its surrounding and hence also its spectators. Participatory Art, on the other hand, *gives the spectator an opportunity for her/his creativity to be used* in the *here and now*, just like the artist uses her or his creativity in preparing the creative moment.

At the end of his book *The Modern Ideal*, published 2005, Paul Greenhalgh, former head of research at the Victoria and Albert Museum in London, claims that "a common critique of the current state of things, …points to the crises in the arts being caused by fragmentation of culture. Modern conditions seem to have undermined the consistency of existence where it can no longer generate a cultural fabric that has any form, depth or longevity; it is as though we live in a cacophony of a million competing and arbitrary sound-bites, dvd clips and internet connections; that we have created a universe in which we have created millions of beads, but have had the thread taken away from us."

Since we live in an extremely fragmented world, I believe the future belongs to those who can combine and recombine, assemble and reassemble something at least individually meaningful out of all those fragments. This is what creativity is all about.[16] Participatory Art wants to highlight this creative capacity within each individual.

Mondrian wrote in 1936: "Nonfigurative art is created by establishing *a dynamic rhythm of determinate mutual relations* which *excludes the formation of any particular form.* We note thus, that to destroy particular form is only to do more consistently what all art has done."[17] (Mondrian's italics). Participatory Art can be seen as a logical next step along that road when we swap the word "destroy" for the word "free". This means freeing the spectator from any particular form rather than destroying any form. Mondrian also used the term "freeing"– when he wrote about an art that "frees itself from the oppression of particular form, thus showing relationships" and "freeing line and color from particular form".[18]

Some well known 20th century artists created one or a few artworks in the vein of Participatory Art, however, they did not use that particular description for their works. Neither did they focus on something in the vein of Participatory Art for any length of time, with the exception of Yaacov Agam around 1950. He called his works in this vein *transformables*. No well known artist has been dedicating their work exclusively to anything like Participatory Art. Lacking an established nomenclature, art in the vein of Participatory Art sometimes sailed under the flag of Kinetic Art, and sometimes ended up as part of the Multiples movement. Lazlo Moholy-Nagy in the 1930s and Joseph Beuys in the 1970s were natural candidates for developing the theory and practice of Participatory Art, given both artists' dictum that everyone is an artist, but neither of them did so. So far, Participatory Art has in fact lived a rather anonymous life.

Some obstacles to Participatory Art

We can only speculate about why there were many tentative beginnings for Participatory Art, but no significant expansion. Maybe the world was not ready for it, in the sense that this art did not reflect its time until now. Another possible reason may be that, as with Conceptual Art, Participatory Art does not fit in with existing market-related art structures that depend heavily on signed and preferably one-off pieces. In contrast, Participatory Art is very much about process - not least the physical process - of the creative moment. Hence it is almost impossible to introduce Participatory Art through verbal expression, as with Conceptual Art, or through still pictures, as with Land Art.

A further obstacle to the expansion of Participatory Art is that such an art work is nearly impossible to sign, because the work of art is not completed without the spectator's participation. Then, how would you sign it and who would sign it? Furthermore, how do you exhibit the art without people walking away with its pieces? These problems have to be solved. However, nothing is impossible, and in any event, those obstacles are external or practical ones.

The internal or psychological obstacles may be even more difficult to overcome. One obstacle may be the artist's ego. An artist bent on expressing him/herself, or becoming famous, may be less attracted to routinely inviting other people to complete the work of art, and thus sharing in the result for better or for worse. What exactly would the artist like to be known for? In addition there is the social isolation of working in a manner that even very few artist colleagues appreciate or even accept.

Yet another obstacle for the development of Participatory Art has all along been that it is very hard to make money out of Participatory Art. Without signatures, and com-posed of several pieces difficult to sign, the Participatory

Art work becomes an uncertain investment for the speculatively inclined art buyer. Such artworks will only sell for a low retail price. This in turn implies serial production of Multiples and the creation of a distribution chain. If you are an artist, this is probably not what you feel like investing your time and energy in. Nor would you necessarily have the talent for it.

An additional problem is that much of Participatory Art probably is abstract sculpture. Both abstract art and sculpture mostly have had a small following. In this way, Participatory Art is a bit like poetry – the poetry of the creative moment.

Toward a Manifesto.

So what, then, is Participatory Art? How does it differ from other kinds of art? Does it have a future?

Participatory Art is radically different from other forms of art in *its exploratory focus*, *its ambitions* and *its means*. Please note, however, that Participatory Art is neither against any other kind of art, nor does it seek to replace other kinds of art. To give you a brief summary, here follows my suggestions for a Manifesto:

1. Participatory Art *is about* exploring, within an aesthetic context, the many emotional facets of *the creative moment* as such and of *one's own creativity*; as opposed to solely contemplating the results of other people's creative moments and creativity.

2. Participatory Art *has its exploratory focus*, not

on line, color, or form per se, not on light or texture, not on narrative or representation, not on still life or the human figure or on landscape, but on the very basis for all art: on *creativity* as such and on the feeling-thinking nature of creativity, as well as on what happens in the creative moment itself.

3. Participatory Art *consists*, technically speaking, of a number of parts/elements (whether physical or electronic) which the "spectator" can (re)arrange, (re)assemble, or (re)combine into whatever whole that the spectator finds interesting – aesthetically or otherwise.

4. Participatory Art *builds on* the relations between its parts/elements/forms and on the changing of those relations on a trial and error basis to suit one's own satisfaction as a "spectator". Participatory Art also builds on the relationship between those parts and the choices made by an individual, thus involving intuition and individual responsibility.

5. Participatory Art *changes the role of the spectator* dramatically – from a relatively passive role of contemplating in front of an object and/or "completing the work of art in ones mind," to a distinctly more active role; not only in the sense that the spectator gets physically involved, but in particular also in that the spectator has to make strategic *choices* for the full work of art to come into being.

6. Participatory Art retains the *artist's task* as intended "to make forms and colors living and capable of arousing emotions" (Mondrian 1937) while at the same time intending to give space to the creativity, physical involvement, and experience of the "spectator".

7. Participatory Art *enables the expression* by the activated "spectator" of a combination of intellectual expression (making strategic *choices*), aesthetic desires (completely contrary to Duchamp's ambitions), and a sensuous experience (in touching, picking up, and moving the various parts of the Participatory Art work).

8. Participatory Art probably most often *manifests itself as* some kind of abstract sculpture, but that is not the only option. Moholy-Nagy and Öyvind Fahlström, for example, experimented with other ways of making art, including pictures that were partially or potentially participatory.

9. Participatory Art *contains* a unique measure of quality. A successful work of Participatory Art is judged also by the extent to which it makes space for the active choices made by the "spectator" for the work of art coming into being.

10. Participatory Art is *founded on* a vision of human creativity being intrinsically of great interest and so in itself worth pursuing for

people in order to gain a deeper understanding of what it means to be a human
being.

Some comments in relation to the Manifesto

The focus on creativity by itself makes Participatory Art
highly relevant for our time, where the entire production
system more and more is characterized by competition
through new ideas rather than through price and
production excellence (both nowadays just taken for
granted).

The making of art by (re)arranging, (re)assembling, or
(re)combining chosen elements into whatever whole
that the person creating finds interesting – aesthetically
or otherwise has previously been reserved for the artists
themselves, as in the geometrical forms used in the Cubi-
series of sculptures by the American artist David Smith
(early 1960s); also in the more abstract forms used in
the *Collages* of George Braque and Pablo Picasso as well
as Max Ernst, Kurt Schwitters and other Dadaists in
the first decades of the 1900s. Later on, a step further
was taken in the *Assemblages* of Louise Nevelson and
perhaps brought to its height by Robert Rauschenberg.
His *Combines* from 1954-1964 seems to extol the joy of
combining, a pleasure still reserved for the artist, though.
Anish Kapoor is quoted as saying "The most important
thing that one is doing is making a transformation".[19]

Yet, both Rauschenberg and Kapoor left the spectator to
be a passive witness to the artist's own transformations.
Conceptual Art in the 1960s took the role of the spectator
in the completion of the work of art one step further than

what art had done before, but it was still within rather defined limits, not as open-ended as in Participatory Art. Conceptual Art seems to have been more focused on the participation by the spectator in *the execution* of a work thought out by the artist and thus not opening up as much space for the creativity of the spectator/participant as in Participatory Art.

Participatory Art *builds on* relations of the various kinds mentioned above and thus also on the spectator/participant's intuition and individual responsibility. Universal beauty arises from "the mutual relations of form", Mondrian wrote in 1937. Furthermore, Mondrian said that "...forms create relations and that relations create forms," and that "the culture of particular form is approaching its end. The culture of determined relations has begun." Participatory Art is *an expression of the next phase – the culture of undetermined, constantly changing relations* as, for example, in human networks. Now, in the new millennium, our culture already finds itself at this point of development or at least seems to be heading in this direction.

Joseph Beuys (following a tradition that goes back to Duchamp and even to Plato) claimed in the 1970s that "everyone is an artist". But his production was not entirely aligned with that conviction. His "signature" lay in the material he frequently used, like felt and fat, rather than in the execution of his art. Participatory Art takes a more definitive step. As opposed to Dadaism which sought to provoke or even alienate the spectator, Participatory Art invites the spectator to contribute her or his own creativity in order to experience it, and to experience creativity in general. In a way it could be argued that the end result is yet another step in Art's millennia-long quest for realistic communication.

Participatory Art challenges not only the spectator/participants intellect and intuition in the strategic choices to be made but also in the physical involvement needed to fulfill the Participatory Art work. The gesture of arms – flexing the elbow, to be specific – needed to move the parts in Participatory Art, is one of the most fundamental movements of human beings. We use this very movement for picking up a baby and for picking food. Participatory Art brings us closer than any other art to the fundamentals of being a human being. Umberto Eco's concept Open Work barely takes into consideration the creativity of the "spectator". It is thus more creator/artist/producer-focused than participator-focused.

Creativity is an expression of a basic human state of mind as well as a basic human activity. "It is only in being creative that the individual discovers the self" according to the famous psychoanalyst D.W. Winnicott.[20]

In what way different?

Why, has art over the centuries explored shape, color, light, structure, as well as the landscape and the human body and face, but not the uniquely human process underlying all art – the creative moment? Why has art banned its own source as a subject matter to be explored?

Painter and sculptor Jean Tinguely created machines with mechanical arms around the middle of the 20ᵗʰ cnetury. At the pressing of a button, these arms would start drawing something non-figurative on a white piece of board.[21] By holding up this joke mirror, Tinguely seemed to pose the question "So you think everything can be mechanized, even the creative act?" But he did not pursue this track any further.

In its earliest versions in the 1960s and 1970s, Participatory Art, just like Pop Art, set out to explore something. Pop Art set out to "explore the material reality of the urban environment."[22] Participatory Art has also tried to explore something, but something very different and over much longer time, and without a cohesive movement with public figure heads and theoretical underpinnings. This essay is an effort to begin to remedy this absence of theory, though I do not claim to cover the entire field that seems vast in time, geography and scope.

Art historian professor Dario Gamboni published in 2002 an impressive and highly scholarly book titled *Potential Images*. Here, Gamboni discusses ambiguity and indeterminacy in modern art and how this has been used by some painters to involve the participation of the spectator. Gamboni focuses on the participation of the spectator's *imagination* in the work of art[23] – the spectator as an "interpreting subject"[24]. I will further explore this form of art in the section on Participatory Art and painting/pictures. Participatory Art, in contrast, is about the *physical participation* of the spectator/participant in the work of art coming into being. In the kind of art that Gamboni describes, the focus is on perception, cognition and imagination. In Participatory Art the focus is on the experience of the *creative moment* and the challenge of the participants' own creativity. Participatory Art can also be seen as an answer to the century-old conflict between collectivism and individualism, and a social construct that is the opposite of alienation, without seeking recourse in the anti-industrialism of Morris and Adorno.[25]

Participatory Art also relates to the fragmentation of today's globalized, instant, and through Internet, totally decentralized culture. In this extremely fragmented culture people highly value the possibility to quickly – preferably instantaneously – (re)combine and (re) assemble new entities out of existing fragments.

In one sense all art is, of course, participatory. As Paul Greenhalgh put it "...by conceiving of the possibility of art, we bring it into existence."[26] To me, the worst enemy of art is indifference and passivity. In all art, the intention is to elicit some kind of response from the spectator/participant, be it an emotional response like awe, admiration, or anger; or even some kind of physical response where the spectator positions him/herself to see better. Sculpture, for example, has always gained from being viewed from different angles. I believe the simplification process inherent in the pioneering work by Cezanne, Matisse, and Kandinsky enabled more of the completion to be achieved by the spectator, even though this might have gone beyond the spectator's expectations.

Some similarities with other kinds of art

Assemblage as an art form was rewarded its own exhibition in 1961 at the Museum of Modern Art in New York.[27] However, contemporary artists like David Smith, Rickard Stankiewics and Louise Nevelson were at the center of attention because of the end results of their art, not because of the actual process of assembling the art pieces, with its hidden drama of strategic choices. In Participatory Art, the focus is on the subjective experiences during the process of assembling and re-assembling.

In his teachings, Paul Klee stressed the *intuitive* moment, according to Norbert Schmitz[28]. Particularly as an instigation, the intuitive moment comes close to, but is not identical with, the *creative* moment. Klee was definitely interested in the act of creating, but his art speaks only of his own creativity and does not invite the creativity of the spectator. Evidently, Klee did not practice Participatory Art.

In many ways, Minimalism (or "literalist" art, as Michael Fried called it) can be said to constitute the end of Modernism in art. Thus, it is of a particular interest to take a look at a conversation between Donald Judd (even though he did not consider himself a minimalist) and Frank Stella, in 1964. Stella says what motivates him when making art is a desire to see how things actually look when they have been completed. Judd concurs that you can think forever about what you wish to make, but it does not exist until it becomes visible. What he desires is to see what he has made.[29] Note that neither of them talks about the joy of creating! The desire to see one's thought materialize is probably a universal human phenomenon. But how can this desire, this joy, be handled in art, if art is only about showing what others have finished?

Donald Judd also said that art is what you look at. Participatory Art does not stop at that. I claim that Participatory Art is also *what you experience when practically working with the materials provided by the artist* and seeing the process unfold, as well as eventually seeing a result that is to your satisfaction. The result, however, is definitely secondary to the experience of the process of creating (but not manufacturing). Incidentally, ranking experience higher than end result mirrors a contemporary development in marketing, where customer *satisfaction* is not an end goal in itself, but customer *experience* has become a much more interesting object of study. Michael Fried, reading Robert Morris, commented that "The object, not the beholder, must remain the center or focus of the situation; but the situation itself *belongs to* the beholder.[30]" (Fried's italics.) In Participatory Art, neither the object nor the beholder is in focus, but the very *act of creating* as such, as experienced by "the beholder" in action. Participatory Art *gives the spectator a creativity to be used,* just as the artist has her or his creativity to use.

The site-specific Minimalist Art of the 1960-1970s created art that existed not only as a relationship between spectator and work of art, but now also included the site, the locale.[31] Similarly, Participatory Art can be described as a relationship between the artist, the end result, and the spectator's actual involvement of her/his creativity. While site-specific art certainly builds on the spectator being present on the spot[32], this presence is still a rather passive act. I doubt that the spectator experiences her/his own creativity at that moment.

Now, at the beginning of the 21st century, with the globalization of communication and the rapid development of technology, I find creativity more than ever a core issue in western societies. If people in the western countries want to maintain their standard of living, while faced with low-cost labor in Asia, they will have to accept the mobilization of their citizens' creativity in both product and process development. We know things are not standing still in Asian countries. China plans to double its Research & Development spending by 2020, compared with 2002, measured as a percentage of Gross National Product (GNP).

In art, keeping the focus on the process of creativity rather than the results of creativity continues to be a problem. Participatory Art, in my mind, is the only art form that specifically addresses the nature of the creative process *while it is occurring*, and does so by specifically building on the engagement of *the spectator/participant's own creativity*. The process is similar to the process where Calder used the immaterial quality of physical balance as part of his Mobiles. Participatory Art is the art where the spectator has to leave his/her traditional role of being predominantly passive and actively enter an open-ended creative process in order to experience what this art fundamentally is about.

Gustav Metzger wrote his first Manifesto for an Auto-Destructive Art in1959. In his art he focused mostly on the act of destruction. A kind of art-in-transition or process art. Guy Debord and the Situationist-movement stressed "decomposition" – self-destruction of traditional forms of culture – in their texts from 1958[33]. Now it is high time that we focus also on the creativity and the creative potential of the individual, is it not?

By definition, Participatory Art requires a radical change in the role of the spectator. The spectator needs to leave his or her fairly passive/meditative role and instead become an active agent, making choices and taking risks, if only aesthetic ones. Participatory Art thus represents a shift from perception of someone else's end result to the actual process of "the spectator's" experience of his/her own creativity.

Making choices and taking risks are at the very core of creativity and the basis of all innovative art. Participatory Art builds also on the individual *creativity of the spectator*, just like ordinary painting builds on the use of canvas, pigment, and a medium. Not everyone is prepared to join in, however, and particularly, not on demand. I would not be surprised if behind that hesitance lies the fear of risking one's vulnerable self-image. The sheer novelty of this new role for the spectator in the work of art may also cause the spectator to hesitate. In a sense, Participatory Art invites a new page to be written in *the history of the art spectator*. Although the history goes back at least to Classical Greece, it is a long history with very few chapters written, so far.

In a speech, Marcel Duchamp, considered one of the most radical artists of the 20th century, reduced the role of the spectator to that of almost refining "as pure sugar from molasses" the real art, to be found somewhere in between the intentions of the artist and the results of her/his execution of the work of art. This happened as recently as in 1957! In the same speech, given in Houston, Texas, Duchamp also said "*The creative act* takes another aspect when the spectator experiences the phenomenon of transmutation; through the change from inert matter into a work of art, an actual transubstantiation has taken place, and *the role of the spectator* is to determine the weight of the work on the aesthetic scale" (my italics). Notice how Duchamp here focuses on the importance of the piece of art coming into being, but also degrades the spectator to the role of a passive spectator cum arbiter of the outcome of the *artist's own process*. "All in all," Duchamp continued, "*the creative act is not performed by the artist alone*; the spectator brings the work in contact with the external world by deciphering and interpreting its inner qualifications and thus adds his contribution to the creative act. This becomes even more obvious when posterity gives its final verdict and sometimes rehabilitates forgotten artists." (My italics.)[34] Duchamp's spectator role is more like reading a novel than engaging in Participatory Art.

The role here ascribed to the spectator, by Duchamp, is still the role of the onlooker in a mute contemplation of the art object, however not entirely passive. Perhaps the role of the spectator is even a bit creative, but only in a cerebral and/or emotional way. Definitely, the spectator is not practically participating. Yet, from the work of people like Piaget and Seymour Papert we now know that precisely *the physical participation in creating something* greatly enhances the experience as well as the final subjective outcome for the individual.[35] The very physical-ness of art cannot be experienced in the same way if you are only a maker, or only a spectator.

The challenge for the Participatory Art artist

At the core of Participatory Art lies the creativity of the individual, located both in the artist and in the participant/spectator. The challenge for the Participatory Art artist is how to release this creativity in both these aspects.

Theoretically, you could give someone a few colored pieces of paper and let them fall through the air down onto a white surface, as did indeed Hans (Jean) Arp in 1916-17.[36] Carl Andre did something similar 50 years later with his "scatter piece" *Spill* in 1966: Around 800 white plastic blocks were spilt from a canvas bag onto the gallery floor, making accidental patterns. Richard Serra's molten lead piece called *Splashing*, created in 1968, is another example of "scatter" art.

You could give someone a lump of clay and ask the person to make something that is aesthetically pleasing to them, out of that. Most people would probably shy away, because they would find the risk of failure overwhelming. In Participatory Art, the role of the artist then may include creating some kind of aesthetic "safety net" along with the experience of aesthetic creation.

In a way, the artist is challenged to invent some kind of material other than raw material for the sole purpose of inviting participants into the process of creating and recreating something with it.

Another challenge for the artist is to create something that is neither so difficult to use that the other person shies away, nor so easy to use that there is no risk of "failure" and hence no challenge. The artist's challenge is to create something aesthetically pleasing and yet not something so finished that there is no room for individual creativity; nor so banal as to be aesthetically uninteresting; nor such that the aesthetical possibilities are severely constrained right from the beginning. A plethora of toys, from Lego bricks to magnetic color strips for the fridge door, would fall into the category of the aesthetically banal. A number of "Executive Toys", usually by anonymous artists or designers but often slightly more ambitious, also fall into the category of the aesthetically banal.

Beauty as such seems to have been pretty much "banned" from the leading edge of art, roughly in the 1960-1990s.[37] Questions thus arise around the use of "aesthetically pleasing" as a motivator in Participatory Art. To some extent "aesthetically pleasing" is simply shorthand for "aesthetically pleasing or in other ways interesting". I have to admit, that in my own work with Participatory Art, aesthetics is a strong motivator. I expect that this is the case also with most spectators/participants using it. Hence, the aesthetics as motivator would form the bridge that connects the artist and the spectator/participant in Participatory Art. Other motivators are also conceivable, for example, simply a wish to exercise one's creativity as such.

How come you have not heard of a Participatory Art before?

If participation is the new name of the game, how come we have not heard of Participatory Art? Has it not yet caught on, and if so, why? After all, participatory toys of various kinds have existed for at least a century. Are we influenced by the exceptional status conveyed on the work of art during Modernism – and by the romantic concept of the artist as an expert or genius? [38]

A simple explanation could be that Participatory Art is not known to have produced a genius and hence has not had a breakthrough in publicity. Another possible explanation is that Participatory Art is not auteur-oriented in a time when "auteur-ship" and stardom are venerated, seemingly more than ever before. In this sense, the artist practicing Participatory Art may be more closely related to pre-Renaissance artists than later ones. Finally, the explanation may be found in the nature of Participatory Art. In itself artistic creativity (meaning non-utilitarian, yet subjectively meaningful creativity) seems to be seen by most people as happening somewhere else, far beyond oneself. This may make people feel more comfortable and may make their lives more convenient. They escape the problems of personal choice with its concomitant risk of failure and hence, personal responsibility.

In the history of art – like in all history of culture – some trends develop so slowly that they can be seen as lasting changes only with great hindsight. I will mention just three trends: the coming and going of an interest in *reality*; the interest in *movement* as such; and the changing relationship between art and *the art spectator.*

Many novel ideas (as opposed to novel products) tend not to catch on immediately. In fact, many novel ideas do not catch on for quite a while. Being novel means to some extent redefining what art is, and most people seem to have strong preconceptions and mindsets about art and resent having them suddenly changed.

Participatory Art is by nature transitory and that may work against its acceptance by a wider public. If art is the open process rather than the end result, how do we exhibit it without mostly showing the by-product – the end result – rather than the main aspect, the process of creating? Indeed, the showing of Participatory Art needs to be different from the exhibition of other kinds of art.

The nature of Participatory Art works against itself also when it comes to distribution within the art world. Participatory Art is a process, thus the outcome cannot be signed. Nor is there much point in producing on-off pieces or limited editions. That would put a limitation on creativity and thus be counter to what Participatory Art stands for. Without objects or processes in their end state, without limited editions and without signatures it is difficult to develop the big names that media build on. Where would the appeal be for those crucial, practical definers of art – the wealthy art collectors? How could this kind of art attract well-established art galleries? What would the art museums display? Would it be counter to their missions to exhibit open-ended processes?

Participatory Art in a brief historical perspective

Did anyone yet write about the changing *history of the art spectator*? To my knowledge, so far, this has not been done. The history of the art spectator is rarely mentioned. Why not? Most likely, the reason is that the history of the art spectator is such a slowly unfolding history spread out over several millennia and hence lacks the sudden shifts that makes the history of art – in particular during the past 150 years – so spectacular. The many novel shifts in the history of art, represented by the various "isms", do not result in equally novel shifts in the role of the spectator. The history of art and the history of the art spectator are not parallel.

With Modernism and Post-Modernism, an interest in

the involvement of the spectator has slowly, (very slowly, indeed!) been growing and taken on many diverse forms: from the blending of the impressionist colors in the spectator's head to figuring out the implementation of the idea, as in Conceptual Art. In between we find phenomena such as Op-Art and various forms of electronically based interactive art.[39]

The more active role of the art spectator has been explored before, but at the time it was hardly noticeable. It was not seen for what it was. This exploration happened at an early stage in Modernism, as we will see in the next chapter. For reasons unknown, the active role of the art spectator did not develop on its own. Maybe the time was not right. A number of other revolutionary developments in art appeared simultaneously. Surely, as millions of people perished, having been commanded to war with one another, we were not living in the "Age of Participation"!

Why do some artists come into contact with something new, yet never cross over into it? Take the late Paul Cezanne[40] and late Monet[41] at the beginning of the 20th century as an example, or Picasso and Braque, who almost became abstract painters during their early cubist years[42] – they all turned away from it. Henri Matisse produced a few semi-abstract paintings already around 1914, but never pursued that idea further. However, toward the end of his life, he returned to near-abstract art in some of his cut-outs. Max Ernst, in 1922, and Lazlo Moholy-Nagy, in the 1930s, touched into the field of Participatory Art, without ever using the term, but again, never pursued it further.

The invention of the foreshortening technique in Classical Greece and the interest in realism among its artists was certainly a dramatic shift in the history of art as well as a shift in what was expected of the art spectator. The ensuing illusionism and idealism can be seen as radical breaks from the past, within the history of art, but hardly implied radical changes in the demands on the spectator. The shift in the history of art represented by the European Middle Ages, discarding realism/illusionism and replacing it with a demand on the spectator to respond with the right emotions of awe and veneration, represents another significant shift in both the history of art and the history of the art spectator. The invention of the central perspective during the Renaissance was a huge shift in the history of art. Yet, I believe it did not represent an equally large shift in the history of the spectator. Was it not merely, as the name Renaissance implies, a revival of something similar that had existed before?

And what about Impressionism? Certainly, it brought about a dramatic change in the history of art, but can the same be said about its impact on the history of the art spectator? As in the case of central perspective, Impressionism placed radically new demands on the perceptions of the spectators, in blending the many colors, visible at closer range but not at a distance. The blending of the paints took place in the brains of the spectators, provided that they acquiesced to positioning themselves at the correct distance from the paintings in order to "get it". They had to physically move themselves until they found the right position. This demand on the spectators' physical movements was indeed something novel, but seems to have been overlooked in the turbulence that the treatment of color caused in the world of art. Furthermore, Impressionism demanded of the spectator a change of focus in yet another sense. From simply looking at something in a meditative way, spectators now had to focus on their own process of seeing (as did Cézanne), and how relative it was, depending on light, time of day (for example, Monet's Haystacks 1891). Fundamentally, Impressionism asked the spectators to take a new interest in reality as such, rather than in idealized versions of reality. Matisse took a step further when he declared that he was not painting what he saw, but what he felt in front of what he saw. Where did that leave the spectator? This was a radicalization of an existing challenge for the spectator, rather than the radically new challenge that came with Cubism and Dadaism.

This shift from the view to the viewer, from the seen to the seeing itself, reached a new climax in the history of art during the latter part of the 19th century, with the advent of Impressionism, Symbolism and Synthesism, as pointed out by Dario Gamboni. These developments paved the way for Cubism, with its more explicit inclusion of the viewer, and for the profound questioning of the multi-faceted process of seeing, initiated by Cézanne.

"The key concept underlying Cubism is that the essence of an object can only be captured by showing it from multiple points of view simultaneously."[43] Thus, we may conclude that Cubism made a historically novel claim on the spectator in asking the spectator to look out for the essence of things, by trying to see them from multiple viewpoints simultaneously.

Something similar happened with the Post-Impressionism

beginning in the 1880s, in particular the Synthesism[44] of Paul Gauguin. Synthesism "substituted traditional recessional space with juxtaposed flat planes of color". [45] The artist's focus shifted away from nature to something inside the artist, as Gauguin put it: "Some advice: do not paint too much after nature: Art is an abstraction; derive this abstraction from nature while dreaming before it, and think more of the creation which will result than of nature. *Creating like our Divine Master is the only way of rising toward God*"[46] (My italics). Odilon Redon was another artist of the same time period emphasizing similar ideas and influencing Duchamp.[47]

Synthesism was an important step in the history of the spectator. Perhaps, Synthesism was on par with the demand to see beyond the foreshortening technique that now appeared obsolete; the demand to fall for the seduction of the illusory effects of central perspective; or the demand to respond with the "right" emotions of awe and veneration when faced with medieval art.

I wonder if Synthesism is the first recorded case of an artist putting the act of creating above everything else. Gauguin, then, would precede Participatory Art with almost a century. We need to remember, however, that unlike Participatory Art, Gauguin still emphasized the creativity of the artist, not the creativity of the spectator.

Only a few decades later, with the advent of Dadaism, a new revolution in art occurred and even greater demands were placed on the spectator. But at the time, not so surprisingly, everyone's focus was on the revolutionary movements as such, rather than on the changing role of the spectator. Nevertheless, there is the parallel perspective of the spectator's role undergoing change.

Since the breakthroughs of Cubism and Dadaism there has been many "isms", but none that changed the demands on the spectator as those two did. On the other hand, some changes in art have put equally radical new demands on the spectator, yet these were not bunched together into an "ism". Abstract art took off around 1912 with artists such as Kandinsky, Vladimir Tatlin, František Kupka , Fernand Léger, Mondrian, Delauney, Malevich, Arp, possibly out of synthetic Cubism. To this day, artists are continuing to create abstract art. Yet, why have we heard of Cubism and Modernism, but not of "Abstractism?"

Furthermore, why did several well known artists come close to abstract art – creating art we may now see as semi-abstract – but why did they not explore it fully? Explorations into abstract art included a few paintings by Cézanne and Monet, around 1900, art by Gauguin, Moreau, Redon , and Seguin as well as some of the pioneering cubist works of Picasso and Braque from the period 1908-1909. Why did these artists not engage fully in abstract art, like some of their cubist followers?

If we had the answers to those questions we might be able to understand why Participatory Art has not yet developed into an "ism", which would make it better known. Could it be that only now, the time has come for this art form – the art of the Age of Participation – an art that now finds itself where abstract art was around 100 years ago, but without manifestos and famous names to market it? Participatory Art has its own antecedents obscured however by perennial flashy trends and the fashions of the day. In trying to understand Participatory Art we may well ask, what prevented so many artists in the early modern movement to engage in abstract art? With so many radical artists active throughout the period of Modernism, why did no one build a career using the phenomenon of *active spectator participation*? Several artists made tentative efforts, a few tried it out, but no one specialized in it, as will be demonstrated throughout the next few chapters.

PART II

HISTORICAL ROOTS BEFORE WW II

The roots of Participatory Art in the early years of Modernism – the first decades of the 20th century.

What moment in history can be seen as the starting point for the history of Participatory Art? One natural starting point is the turn of the last century. At that time, artists held opposing views of art and the artist. Ruskin, William Morris, and Jugend represented one approach, and Walter Gropius and the German Werkbund and later Bauhaus and Funktionalism, represented another approach.[48] Though these conflicting views of art certainly paved the way for Participatory Art, it was more in the way of creating fertile ground than constituting roots, as was the progressive pedagogy of those days, on the whole[49].

Other starting points for the history of Participatory Art could be the shift away from realistic rendering, in favor of the Cubism of Picasso and Braque, around 1907; or the pioneering of abstract painting by Kandinsky and Kupka, around 1910. Yet, neither of these turns in the history of art paved the way for the subsequent slow development of Participatory Art to quite same extent as did the Dada movement and in particular Marcel Duchamp, one of the leading persons of that movement. If anyone can be said to personify the roots (even if only the roots) of Participatory Art, it would have to be Duchamp. This shift in art history took place through what I believe must have been something of a personal crisis, that he went through during 1912-13, at the age of 25.

Marcel Duchamp and the early roots of Participatory Art

In 1911, Duchamp decides to begin painting in the profoundly new cubist manner, pioneered a few years earlier by Picasso and Braque. The result is the attractive painting *Portrait de joueurs d'échecs* (The Chess Players). "I decided to paint in a cubistic way... I wished to live in the present and the present in those days was Cubism", he is quoted as saying.[50] During January 1912 Duchamp paints the now famous *Nu descendant un éscalier II* (Nude Descending a Staircase II). In this painting, Duchamp is trying to apply Cubism to movement – a radical novelty at that time. "But if I wish to show how an airplane takes off, I will try to show what it is doing, I will not paint a still life" he says[51]. In February 1912 Duchamp submits his painting to the Salon des Indépendants in Paris. But, to what must come as a great surprise to him – his two artist brothers are, after all, on the committee – his fellow cubists in the hanging committee do not wish to have his painting included in the exhibition! They ask him to at least paint over the title. Duchamp refuses and instead withdraws his painting.

The Swedish art critic Ulf Linde, who knew and worked with Duchamp in the 1960s (Duchamp died in 1968), wrote that Duchamp would later often refer to this rebuttal with great bitterness. Though the event did not mark the definite end to Duchamp's cubist painting, it came close to ending it. Duchamp now embarked on a different journey. Rather than occupying himself with the problem of perception and rendering of outer reality, he turned inward. In a series of more or less abstract works of art,[52] and in approximately 100 notes[53], he gradually, over the span of several years, built up the different parts of a very complex and almost entirely abstract painting on glass, which he painted between 1915, when he had moved to New York and 1923. This famous painting, variously called *La Mariée mise à nu par ses célibataires, même* (The Bride Stripped Bare by Her Bachelors, Even) or The Large Glass, has become an emblematic painting of abstract art and of the modern movement in general.

The origins of this emblematic painting seems to be an experience Duchamp had during a visit to his parents in Rouen over Christmas and New Year 1911-1912, at age 24. Duchamp had stopped in front of a chocolate manufacturer's window, one he had gazed through as a child. Through the window he saw a large chocolate blender milling around in an endless circular *movement*. In the window pane, Duchamp also saw his own face reflected. I believe that, at this particular moment, in this particular place, a number of questions surfaced simultaneously in the mind of the young Duchamp. His questions may have been: "What is reality, really?" And: "Who am I in this reality – the surface or that which is below the surface? Am I what I can see or what is behind what I can see? If so, what is that? Could the chocolate blender be *perceived* both as a machine and as a symbol for mechanical or biological drives, or something more? Does the perceiver simultaneously perceive the surface and the underlying reality – the whole? Or am I the agent reflecting on the whole situation and thereby, in fact, *bringing something to that which I am looking at and thereby creating something new*? What is the role of *chance* in all this? Has this 'chance' brought all these things together at this very moment?"

After all it is by chance that Duchamp is standing there, seeing at that particular moment what he is seeing and thinking what he is thinking. Is he also a young man just by chance? And what is this *creativity*, that urges him to combine all these thoughts and perhaps also to render this very visual, multifaceted situation in one picture? Or is he, in reality, just awareness as such? The great French philosopher Bergson had, after all, in 1907 published his much respected book *L'évolution créatrice*. It seems that almost all the questions that would later occupy Duchamp until the end of his life, were experienced by him in that one defining moment in front of the chocolate maker's shop window in Rouen.

No wonder that Duchamp, feeling rebutted by his fellow cubists, set out on a new artistic course. In 1915, he moved to New York. The reason for his move was not to avoid the draft (he had a heart problem and would not be drafted) but he felt that there was no room for him in Paris because Picasso, Braque, and others were hogging the limelight. Duchamp remained in New York until February 1923. Besides painting his huge glass painting *La Marieé...* and playing a leading role in the New York version of the Dada movement, Duchamp notably developed his famous *Ready-mades,* where he further explored *the role of chance* as well as *the role of the spectator in a work of art.* This, precisely, made him an early forerunner to what would several decades later develop into Participatory Art.[54]

Ready-mades and Participatory Art

For many people Marcel Duchamp is synonymous with the provocative exhibition of everyday objects – a rack for drying bottles, a porcelain urinal turned on its back, a snow shovel – and calling it art. (The famous bicycle wheel turned upside down on a stool, however, was not originally created to be a *Ready-made.*)[55] To believe that Duchamp just wanted to be provocative is a mistake. By exhibiting these objects as art Duchamp wished to highlight the *subjectivity* of our perception of reality. He pointed out the fact that we all bring something of ourselves to the observations we make. To provide a demonstration of this process for scrutiny and debate, he felt he had to start with something as neutral as possible – to find, preferably by chance, an everyday object that could be found anywhere. He chose an object that had no intrinsic meaning, not even beauty, to anyone, except for the function it was designed for. Then, Duchamp would empty that object even of any last fragment of meaning, by extracting it from its normal context and placing it into a context where it had absolutely no meaning, such as in an art gallery. Only then would people be free to experience the process of how they attributed meaning to these objects, thus turning them into art objects. With this kind of art, Duchamp demonstrated the fact that spectators do bring something to anything they look at, also to any work of art; just as he himself had found meaning in the image of the chocolate blender, a few years earlier, in that shop window in Rouen.

The radically new aspect of the *Ready-mades* was not just the entry of everyday objects into the art world, shocking as this was to most people. The radically new elements of the *Ready-mades* were mainly two; one was the *role of chance in a work of art*; the other was *the participating role of the spectator*. Duchamp, through his *Ready-mades,* made both of these roles the center piece of his art. In doing so, he, of course, preceded Participatory Art. However, for reasons I will come back to examine later, we cannot say that Duchamp was creating Participatory Art at this time. Suffice it here to point out that Duchamp was still fundamentally exploring *perception* as such. He was not particularly interested in the creative potential of either the spectator or of the creative act itself.

The role of chance in art

There is no doubt that chance played an important role in Duchamp's kind of art. To the philosopher Nietzsche, chance was extremely important; and Duchamp had read Nietzsche's writings. Was it not, after all, chance that led Duchamp to the profound experience he had in that chocolate maker's shop window in Rouen? Even some of the details he used for *La Mariée...* seem to have been created earlier than 1912 and without any particular connection to the final glass painting.[56] Duchamp drew heavily on one art work for *La Mariée...* his *3 stoppages etalon* from 1913-14. This work was a kind of research into the *visualization of chance* and, at the same time, *a work of art with chance being its main focus.* The importance of chance was strongly connected to finding objects that were as empty of meaning as possible. From a Participatory Art point of view, however, the importance of Duchamp's use of chance in art was that he apparently was the first artist to *deliberately relinquish personal control over the end result* of his art. Maximum personal control over the end result would in both cases be contrary to maximizing the spectator option to fill the objects with meaning and hence, contrary to the content of this new kind of art.

Real movement as part of a work of art and Participatory Art

A starting point for *movement in art*, that later would be labeled Kinetic Art or Mobiles, came in 1915, when Marcel Duchamp, in Dadaist fashion, exhibited his famous bicycle wheel, mounted on its fork, turned upside down on a stool. He called it *Roue de bicyclette (Bicycle wheel)* and claimed this object to be art. The wheel could be spinning or not, which is important to remember. At this point in time, there was no demand on the spectator for any physical participation. The mere fact that the artist brought such a mundane object into an art gallery and claimed it to be art was so provocative that it seemed to completely overshadow the fact that *this was also the first time that actual movement* – and not a rendering of it – had been introduced as art, even if that was not the main point of this particular art object, at this particular time.

Needless to say, the *Bicycle Wheel*, and the audacity to

exhibit it as art, provoked the art public – as was indeed intended. But why? Was this uproar only because of the audacity, not to say impertinence, of challenging the conventions of the bourgeoisie, by calling something art, that the contemporary art public could only perceive as definitely non-art or even anti-art? What role did the very *movement* of the bicycle wheel and the potential hands-on-experience play? Did something happen that went deeper than the mere chock effect, something that people at the time perhaps did not notice? I suggest that in putting the label "art" on this object, the artist now *demanded something more of the public* than just accommodation (as the Impressionists had done).

In an interview held June 21st, 1967, a year before Duchamp's death, for the French radio l'ORTF, Duchamp mentioned the *Bicycle Wheel* of 1913 (the 1915 one was a "copy" of the first one) as the first *Ready-made*. But in this interview Duchamp does not mention any participation aspect of this object, though he speaks of the *Kinetic* aspect. "I simply put it on a stool and I looked at it turning, that is, the *movement* was included in the idea of the ready-made and that was one of the first things with movement that I found interesting."[57] (My italics and translation). Note that there is no mention of any specific role for or involvement of the spectator. After all, the spectator's involvement and perception had been a central theme for Duchamp since he painted his cubistic *Nude descending a staircase* in 1912. It is worth noticing that while Duchamp introduced both actual *movement in art* (not just rendering it in a cubist fashion) and, perhaps unintentionally, also introduced *physical participation* (a spectator could set his *Bicycle Wheel* spinning as an *in-*

tegral part of that work of art), he did not pursue either path in his subsequent work beyond the pressing of a button. Duchamp only explored the participation aspect once more, as far as I know, and in a very particular and limited way, when in January 1916 he wrote from New York to his sister Suzanne, a painter in her own right, in Paris, instructing her to choose her own phrase and inscribe it on his ready-made *Bottlerack*,[58] as a deliberate art-creating practice.

The origins of *spectator choice* and Participatory Art

Can we thus conclude that Duchamp's *Bicycle Wheel* was a form of proto-Participatory Art? Judging from Duchamp's own comments at a later date, this is not clear. In his 1957 Houston speech on creativity, Duchamp makes a major point of "the inability of the artist to express fully his intention" and that the struggle of the artist "cannot and must not be fully self-conscious..." And furthermore: "...art history has consistently decided upon the virtues of a work of art through considerations completely divorced from the rationalized explanations of the artist."[59] This statement fits in with the way Duchamp stressed the importance of *the idea content* in a work of art (and thus anticipating Conceptual Art). Besides, *Bicycle Wheel* was later turned into the first ever Ready-made. As such, it stressed not only the importance of the *idea*, but also the importance of *choice*[60] in art, and the relevance of both chance and choice in the making of art. All these aspects are equally relevant to Participatory Art!

The way Duchamp developed his art from the first *Bicycle Wheel in 1913* leads us to believe that Duchamp's *Bicycle wheel* was intended as something in between static sculpture and Mobile Art. Seven years later Duchamp crossed another bridge of sorts. In 1920 he displayed his *Rotative Plaques verre /Optiqu de precision (Rotary Glass Plates/Precision Optiques)*. Duchamp now demanded of the spectator that an electrical button should be pushed so that the glass began to revolve. Here, the first mechanical art object in modern times was on show. Duchamp later followed up this idea with *Rotoreliefs*.[61]

Perhaps it is not surprising that the war years was the time when Duchamp through his several examples of *Ready-made,* explored and manifested the importance of *personal choice* by the spectator in the work of art coming into being – not yet in its physical form – but as a work of art. With his *Ready-mades* Duchamp wanted, amongst other things, to stress the role of *choice* in art just like, for example, the Impressionists had highlighted the role of perception in light and color. Choice had always existed in art - the artist's choice of paint, of canvas, of subject matter etc. With the *Ready-mades,* Duchamp wished to highlight *choice* itself and the role of chance by stressing its importance through its seeming absence. To distill the issue of choice further, Duchamp emphasized that this choice had to be a totally disinterested one: "You choose something that is of no visual interest to the artist. In other words, arrive at a state of mind of indifference to this object. At that moment it becomes a ready-made. If it is something which pleases you....it is aesthetic, it is pretty, you put it in the sitting room. That is not at all the intention of the ready-made." (My translation).[62] I find it interesting to notice that there is absolutely no mention of any of the problems inherent in choice such as necessary trade-offs and individual responsibility; or the fact that by exerting your choice you become to some extent a co-creator of the ensuing results. But then, these were the early days. We do not criticize vintage cars for not matching the design of modern cars.

The major difference between Duchamp's art in 1913 and his art in 1920, is that by 1920, simply looking at the object of art was *not* enough. Now Duchamp expressly demanded of the spectator to *take an initiative*, to *get physically involved* (in this case by pressing a button), that is, to *physically participate,* albeit in a very small way, in the work of art coming into being. Without that initiative by the spectator, that specific work of art would not come into being *as intended by the artist* and hence it would be impossible for the spectator to either fully see or fully experience. The crucial words here are "as intended by the artist", because this differentiates the mechanical variety of Kinetic art, locked in a preset pattern that the spectator can only chose to initiate or not, from Participatory Art.[63] In the latter case there is no end result except the one intended by the spectator/participant. The artist lays down the starting point and perhaps to some extent some rules. Then the choices to be made are left to the spectator/participant.

1920 seems to have been a breakthrough year for movement in art and for participation in art. In 1913, the invitation to participate in spinning Duchamp's *Bicycle Wheel* was eclipsed by the challenge of seeing this particular object as art. Similarly, now in 1920, the sensation of introducing movement in art eclipsed the several instances of also introducing participation in art.

Participation was introduced around 1920 as a result of the Dadaists paving the way. They did it in two ways: By *disclaiming the value of authorship*, renouncing the artist-as-expert role; and by stressing the importance of the spectator's choice (as in the Ready-mades). Participation was still limited – activating something or not activating it, as if the spectator's options were only to say either yes or no – a position most of us resent being in.

By now, I have clarified some of the connections between Participatory Art and Marcel Duchamp. Let us now further explore to what extent there are connections between Participatory Art and the Dada movement in general.

The Dada movement and other early roots of Participatory Art

The emphasis on *personal choice* constitutes a main link between Dada and Participatory Art. The major cause for the divide between the artistic cultures of 1913 and 1920 may be the World War I that left 9 million soldiers dead, and add to that the civilian casualties. From the point of view of Participatory Art it is worth noticing that many Dadaists, when war broke out, were faced with extremely difficult personal choices involving life and death: to enlist or not enlist; and if enlisted, fight the war or try to escape it. Many Dadaists refused to *participate* in the war of their own *choice*. Hugo Ball, for example, volunteered three times, and then turned against the war.

Although we can recognize some early roots of Participatory Art in Dadaism it does not necessarily mean that the former is only a branch of the latter. It means that some of the central characteristics of Dadaism can also be discerned in the much later Participatory Art. Is that enough reason to regard those two as closely related? No. Do they share a philosophy? No. Do they have central values in common? Not really. But Participatory Art and Dadaism share roots in the historical processes: the world wars. They also address certain essential issues such as *creativity* and *play*, and the role of *individual choice* (a sine qua non for Participatory Art), and therefore a special *respect for the individual* – a contrast to the political-economic structures of their time. Both kinds of art, to some extent, also made *the relationship between art and spectator* a central issue. Their respective ways of treating this issue are different, however. Participatory Art, in contrast to Dadaism, always aims to involve the *physical actions* of the spectator whereas the spectator involvement in Dadaism seems to be a question of "forcing the viewer to participate actively in *assembling meaning* – a meaning that insisted on being uncertain and unstable"[64] (my emphasis). In their essay for the catalogue accompanying the great Dadaist exhibition at Centre Pompidou in 2005, Janine Mileaf, and Matthew Witkovski used the expression "participatory theatre" to describe the kind of spectator involvement the Paris Dadaists elicited from their audiences.[65]

Just like Dadaism once was, Participatory Art is now, but in a totally different way, a "radical rethinking of art making", in the words of an expert on Dadaism, Leah Dickerman, describing Dadaism.[66] Dickerman mentions Dada as being "a refusal to 'stay at a distance,' a refusal of both transcendence and sublimation.' Its adherents recognized themselves to be immersed, with no position above or outside that would allow a more reflective view." And she further said: "…also the rejection of art as *illusionistic,* conjuring imaginary worlds."

The same can be said of Participatory Art, except that, in a way that reminds us of Matisse and Calder, there is no rejection of anything, no "anti" anything in Participatory Art, nothing aggressive, and certainly nothing nihilistic in it. Rather, the contrary – Participatory Art is just pro: pro creativity; pro individual choice, and pro activity rather than reflection-only. It empowers the individual rather than attacking existing structures. To be fair, however, it must also be said that some expressions of Dadaism were not only anti-conformist but also pro-something.

Dadaism – again, like Participatory Art – was "an art that cultivated spontaneity, chance, and experiment."[67] Its effort (in itself pro-something) to expand the conventional notions of art (for example, the classical one of illusionism) by including elements like play, "primitive" art and the art of the mentally ill[68] can be seen as further examples of pro-something in Dadaism. Indeed, Dada artists tried to respond to and handle the acutely felt, immense problem of human aggression as experienced by them during WW I. In itself this can be seen as being pro-something, even though we may not always agree with the ways this was done.

Dadaism and Participatory Art have something else in common that both have sought to highlight. This is the phenomenon of *creativity* as such. The Paris Dadaists, in particular, endeavored to do this by striving to "radicalize creativity by opening it up to the mundane, the anonymous, to the spontaneous or the collectively produced."[69]

An interesting turn of Dadaism's ambition to *expand the notion of art* is that the Dadaists did this not only by including whatever material the artist felt like using (rather than the classical oil and gouache paints, fine stone and bronze), but also by using any technique like collages, photomontage, air brush and the use of chance instead of adhering to the classical notion of painting as a pure language of color and form. In removing the artist's hand, they, of course, also often" eliminated the presence of the artist as author of his or her own work."[70] This is often – though not as a principle – also the case in Participatory Art.

Just like Dadaism, one may say that Participatory Art is "not defined by a consistent style". But does Participatory Art instead cohere around a set of strategies like "abstraction, collage, montage, the Ready-made, and the incorporation of chance and forms of automation", as did Dadaism? No, I do not think so. None of the aforementioned strategies are relevant to Participatory Art. If there is a strategy to Participatory Art, it is only that for the participatory work of art to fully come into being, we must make room for the spectator to leave his or her traditionally more passive or reflective role and become an independent, active agent, a participant in the work of art coming into being.

With the advent of industrialism came a natural interest in machines and movement. The fascination with machines enters art prominently with Turner's steam engine and then becomes central in a different manner to Picabia, other Dadaists (especially as man-as-a machine)[71] and the

Russian Constructivists. Movement as such was at the center of interest already for the futurists and cubists.[72] The problem was that their renditions of movement had been static, just like the artists of Classical Greece and Rome struggled with rendering the chariot's wheels in motion. The futurists also tried to render movement as did Marcel Duchamp in 1912.

During the following 10 years of Dadaism, Duchamp and the other Dadaists demanded that the spectators broaden their *concept of the nature of art* (more so than had the cubists and the futurists) to encompass *intellectual ideas* and not only *retinal stimulus* and *manual skills*. Indeed "*art coming into being*", rather than the actual making of art, became a central concern for the Dadaist movement[73]. Duchamp's Ready-mades were only one example.[74] While the role of the artist changed in principle, in this context, in practice it seemed to have continued in the same old vein of the "artist-as-expert."

The commitment of the Dadaists was to *lived experience* and to "*probing experience itself.*" "The artist's task was to move beyond aesthetic pleasure and to affect people's lives; to make them see and experience things differently."[75] To artists, art should also encompass a *transitional concept of art* – art becoming art in the eye of the beholder and/or depending on the context being, say, an art gallery, rather than a hardware store.

At the Cologne Dada Fair in April 1920 Max Ernst showed a sculpture with an axe attached with which to destroy the sculpture/object (which apparently the public also did again and again). As a piece of art this sculpture may not have been particularly great, but it is worth noticing, however, that while this seems to be the first recorded instance of something like Participatory Art when the audience for the first time in the history of art is asked to leave their traditional physical passivity and become active, they are then only asked to either initiate a preset process by pushing (an electrical button, for example) or destroying something already created by someone else. Did this perhaps mirror a view of human nature, tainted by the experiences of WW I, as a mechanical machine? And/or as something inherently destructive – but with the potential of also being creative?

Thus, it seems fair to say that both Duchamp and Max Ernst only in a very limited way sought to engage the creativity of their audience. In my opinion, engaging spectator creativity is the hallmark of true Participatory Art. One possible explanation, built on the Dadaists' penchant for "épater la bourgeoisie" – to shock the middle-classes – is that Duchamp and the other Dadaists thought there was not much creativity in the public at large, to be engaged.[76] Indeed, in general, Dadaism was criticized for its nihilism and for denying the existence of anything such as an intrinsic 'human nature'[77]. Participatory Art, on the other hand, I would say, was founded on a more positive, optimistic view of human nature. However, these few early efforts at participation should perhaps be seen as proto-Participatory Art? Another possible explanation as to why Participatory Art did not flourish out of the Dada movement is that Dadaism was a strong reaction against what its practitioners viewed as the madness of war and the politico-economic powers behind the war. After all the reactions to the war, maybe there simply was not much energy or optimism left for an art founded on the positive concept of the human being? We also need to keep in mind that Freud's rather pessimistic view of the unconscious influenced the Dadaists. An interesting question to ask is, why did Dadaism develop into Surrealism, while there was very little, if any, movement in the direction of increasing spectator involvement?

Around 1920, when Duchamp first displayed his *Rotary Glass*, two new trends were born in the world of art. The first, variously called Kinetic Art or Mobile Art, gradually caught on and developed in two directions – the mechanical Kinetic Art driven by electric motors, wind, or water; and Kinetic art powered exclusively by human actions. The second direction, which I see as leading on to Participatory Art, developed more slowly. At that time, it had not yet built any theory of its own. It had not created a school with a following. It had not caught the eye of major galleries, museums, collectors or critics that together have the power of defining modern art. One may well speculate about the reasons for this "non-development": lack of theory, lack of proximity of the practitioners, lack of commercial sign-able value, lack of readiness of the times. We will return to this issue, but for the sake of the chronology and background of Participatory Art, let us first dwell for a moment on Kinetic or Mobile Art.[78]

Kinetic or Mobile Art opens up for Participatory Art

Compared with the period 1910-1920, the decade that followed saw embryonic forms or proto-versions of Participatory Art. Characteristically, these were geographically scattered and without any conscious theoretical underpinning. They had no established name pushing for the concept, but they appeared more frequently than during the previous decade, partly, it seems, because the new trend of Kinetic Art or Mobile Art opened up new possibilities.

By the early 1920s, the early precursors of Participatory Art were most discernable in New York and Berlin. In both cities they were largely found in connection with *Kinetic sculpture.*

In New York, Kinetic Art was mainly developed by a small group of Europeans who had escaped the war in Europe. The dominant artists were Marcel Duchamp, Francis Picabia, and the American Man Ray. Together they later on came to constitute the core of the Dadaist movement in New York.

The main inspiration for this interest in *the Kinetic work of art* probably came from Duchamp and Picabia (they were friends from pre-war Paris). Duchamp had been interested in Kinetics already when he made his first *Bicycle Wheel* in Paris back in 1913. Though this piece of art clearly had a Kinetic aspect to it – the movement of the wheel – the role of movement as such seems to have been more of a side issue.[79] From *The Bicycle Wheel* Duchamp proceeded for about ten years to develop the concept of the *Ready-made.* The subsequent series of Ready-mades were not Kinetic in themselves, though they could be hung up in the air and made to turn and throw shadows as was done in his retrospective exhibitions in France in 1967. But these effects were not intrinsic to the idea of Ready-mades, according to Duchamp himself.[80].

Picabia, it is worth noticing, had a longstanding and intense interest in depicting machines and things mechanical, starting with his arrival in the United States in 1915.[81], though he was not the only one with such an interest at the time. Another source of inspiration may have been the fellow Dadaist (but Cologne Dadaist) Max Ernst. Around this time (1919) Ernst was working on his series of "diagrammatic collages". At first glance one could mistake them for drawings of machines by an engineer.[82] Ideas traveled fast between the various centers of Dadaism! Closer at hand in New York appeared the paintings of the American architect/painter/photographer Morton Schamberger. A couple of years before his death in 1918, Schamberger created some striking pictures, sometimes called Mechanical Abstraction – a possible inspiration to Pop Art in the 1950s-1960s.

The year 1920 could be claimed to be the year when Kinetic Art really made its debut. Duchamp showed his *Rotary Glass Plates*,[83] the first mechanical work of art in modern times, in which you could see the final art work only if you pressed an electrical button. The button started a machine that rotated pieces of painted glass mounted on a metal shaft. Once again we see how Duchamp included a *participative aspect* to his art; yet it played only a minor role from the point of view of creativity and, yet again, it was not an angle he would pursue later.

In that same year Man Ray showed his *Abat-Jour*, [84] a broad coil of white lampshade material hanging down and moving with the draft *or when someone blew at it*. In 1923 Man Ray created his *Object to Be Destroyed*, a metronome with a photo of an open eye attached to the ticking hand of the metronome as well as his coat hanger mobile *Obstructions*, a series of ordinary coat hangers connected at their ends. This technique was later taken much further by Alexander Calder in his mobiles from the 1930s and onwards. Oddly enough, Man Ray seems to have come to Kinetic Art by ways of photography. Ray was an American painter who eventually became a well-known photographer. In 1920, Ray made a photograph called nothing less than *Moving Sculpture* depicting light colored washing swaying in the wind on a clothesline, against a dark background. Why did Man Ray in 1920 call his still photo *Moving Sculpture* and his moving photo or mobile from 1923 *Object to Be Destroyed*? The words "moving" and "destroyed" are surely the key words here. Note that 1920 was also the year when Ernst at the Cologne Dada Fair showed a sculpture with an axe attached, to be used by the spectator for destroying the sculpture.

We may then conclude that the origins of Participatory Art lies with setting mechanics in motion and with WW I in general – a war in which Duchamp, Ernst and Ray consciously had *chosen* not to join as participants. The very idea of war highlighted that most primitive mode of participation imaginable – *destruction*. Setting mechanics in motion and deciding not to take part in the war both highlighted the extreme importance of *personal choice*. Furthermore, it was during WW I that technology entered warfare on a large scale, with the invention of mobile fire power in the form of tanks, and mass-destructive machines such as machine guns. Yet, at that time, Ray did not see it that way. His emphasis seems to have been on "remaking the object, the object's disappearance and its subsequent reproduction in a new form"[85] – but *through representation in photography rather than in actual life*. But would you not agree that this also mirrored what was happening to the whole society during and after WW I?

In 1932, Ray took another step toward Participatory Art, in that he then "authorized each viewer to construct and obliterate a similar effigy: 'Cut out the eye from the photograph of one who has been loved but is seen no more. Attach the eye to the pendulum of a metronome and regulate the weight to suit the tempo desired. Keep going to the limit of endurance. With a hammer well-aimed, try to destroy the whole in a single blow.'"[86] Again we encounter this "authorization" similar to how Duchamp had authorized his sister in 1916. But again this art represents *de*struction rather than *con*struction.

Constructivism in the 1920s

Parallell to Kinetic Art a more *con*structive note seems to have been struck first in Moscow in 1917 and then in 1920 in Berlin. In Berlin, events similar to developments in New York seems to have taken place, not so much within the Dada movement as within the Constructivist movement. As the name implies, the focus had shifted here onto an interest in *con*struction (primarily in mechanical construction, it seems). Would it be fair to say both movements were slowly, very slowly, opening their eyes to the possibility of participation by the spectator in the work of art coming into being? A difference here is that the Dadaists were strongly influenced by the *de*struction of WW I – not least machines such as the machine gun and the battle tank turned against human beings – while the constructivists in Berlin and Moscow seem to have been more influenced by the challenge of re-construction of a society or construction of a new kind of society along utopian lines; this time incorporating technology and the machine, rather than having them added on to an old society, as life had been, before WW I.

Naum Gabo[87] made his motor powered *Kinetic Construction* in 1920 and about the same time Alexander Rodchenko made his variations on *Hanging Construction*. But how much did Rodchenko care whether the suspended sculpture was set in motion by a spectator, or just by an accidental draft of air? Rodchenko apparently also made "modular sculptures"… "each of which is made of equal-sized woodblocks, the plan sometimes being equal to the elevation".[88] *The Realistic Manifesto* was published by Naum Gabo and his brother Antoine Pevsner in August 1920.[89] It focused explicitly on *movement in art*. In this manifest, Constructivism was first mentioned. The focus was, however, more on the experience that came from *the spectator physically moving* in relation to the work of art – the "idiomotoric movement."[90] This movement was first explored, probably unintentionally,[91] by Duchamp, in his comprehensive work on transparent glass (*La Mariée…* from 1915-23).

Dolls and theater costumes

A special kind of possible precursor to Participatory Art is represented by the work of two women, independent of one another – one belonging to the Zurich and the other to the Berlin Dadaist Movement. Are we to regard Sophie Taeuber-Arp's series of marionette figures (*Marionettes pour* Le Roi cerf *de Garlo Gozzi* made in 1918[92]) as Mobile

Art or just as modern versions of the age-old marionette doll art? If we accept her dolls as a kind of Kinetic Art and possibly also Participatory Art, should we then also regard Matisse's costumes for Diaglev's *Ballet Russe* in 1920 and Oscar Schlemmer's costumes for the *Triadic Ballet* in 1922[93] as Kinetic Art? The answer is probably yes. Yet, from a Participatory Art point of view there is an important difference. The dolls of Sophie Tauber-Arp could in principle be manipulated at will by the "spectator", whereas the spectators at the Ballet Russe or Triadic Ballet remained more passive. Now, what about Hannah Höch's very Dada looking dolls made in 1916?[94] They could certainly be manipulated by the spectator. But they need not be, in order to come into being.

A similar case can be put forward with Alexander Calder's famous *Circus* created in Paris during the years 1926-30. Like the puppet dolls of Arp and Höch, *Circus* can be seen as Participatory Art in its proto-form; a kind of cross-breed between a puppet show, a toy, and a piece of art. *Circus*, like the puppet dolls, could of course also be seen as a static piece of art by their creators, as when *Circus* was displayed in a case of its own at the Calder retrospective at the Witney Museum in 1976. It seems to me, however, that the *Circus* primarily was conceived as part of a performance staged by Calder himself, from time to time, from 1926 onwards, performed the last time in 1976. On the whole, *Circus* seems to have been more akin to a puppet theatre with more of a parallel to the dolls of Sophie Tauber-Arp and Hannah Höch, rather than a form of non-mechanical Kinetic Art. But, when/if someone else was allowed to use the different parts of *Circus* (which seems to have happened at times[95]) the very experience of doing so and whatever reactions it stirred in the user, would have made *Circus* into a work of Participatory Art, provided anyone at that moment had paid attention to this aspect (which I don't think they did). Though, my impression is that this participatory potential was definitely not a conscious and deliberate goal of the artist. Hence, it probably is more appropriate to describe *Circus* as a proto-form of Participatory Art, similar, in this respect, to the *Bicycle Wheel* by Duchamp. Both can perhaps also be regarded as proto-forms of Kinetic Art.

To sum it up: The important observation here is that around 1920, several artists worked with and exhibited Kinetic Art, although none of them were doing so exclusively. Something new had happened in art, apart for the many new isms. The first steps had been taken on a new road. Art had begun to change its relationship with its own audience. *The role of the spectator had begun to change,* from being that of a rather *passive spectator* to that of being an *intended provoké* by provocateurs (Dadaists), to being the *initiator* of planned and *controlled* events (Duchamp et al), to being the initiator of planned but *random* experiences within a planned framework, or, perhaps it is more apt to say, around a planned skeleton of artistic (non-utilitarian) qualities (Ray and Calder). Furthermore, the Dadaists, and Duchamp in particular, had with their art raised the question about the possibilities of *abandoning creative control* and hence also of the *role of authorship* in art, as well as the *role of chance in art.* All three are fundamental aspects also for any theory of Participatory Art.

In the beginning of this essay I discussed the features of the Participation Age of our own time. Exactly these features – abandoning of creative control, as in Open Source technology; the role of authorship in free-ware, contra patents; and the role of chance in inventions – these are at the forefront of IT and business debate today.

The 1930s and the early beginnings of Participatory Art: Alexander Calder, Mobile Art, and the open-ended work of art

The first artist to focus (although not exclusively) on *Kinetic Art* seems to have been Alexander Calder from 1930 and onwards. It all began in the fall of 1930 with Calder paying a visit to Mondrian's Paris studio. Mondrian's studio at this time was almost an installation in itself. On the white walls, Mondrian had put colored rectangles that *he himself* could move around, to make new compositions. Calder, who was an engineer, by training, suggested to Mondrian that "perhaps it would be fun to make those rectangles oscillate?" Mondrian replied that "No, it is not necessary, my painting is already fast."[96] Some years later, in 1943, Mondrian put this put more clearly into words in his last essay as he wrote: "The dynamic movement established by opposition of forms and their colors constitutes the expression of universal reality. In single forms, dynamic movement reveals itself through the continuous opposition of their composing elements: volumes, planes, determined by lines and colors. For this reason, the work appears 'living.'"[97]

The visit to Mondrian's studio in Rue du Départ had a catalytic effect on Calder. He went back home to his own studio and created a few abstract paintings. A few weeks later he turned to abstract sculpture.[98]. Calder got the idea to combine *abstraction* and *movement*. At first, Calder's abstract sculptures were mechanically driven, often by small motors but sometimes by a crank, like his wire sculpture *Goldfish Bowl* in1929, and its parts moving in pre-set patterns inspired by the universe. Then, within a short time, he began utilizing *chance* in the form of random movement. He began creating the kind of abstract Kinetic sculpture that was to become so much of his signature. The earliest examples of Calder Mobiles seems to be *Calderberry Bush* (1932) and *Cône d'ébène* (1933). Both used the random movements of objects moving like pendulums.[99] Duchamp was the first one, in 1932, who called Calder's moving sculptures Mobiles. It may well have been the art of Mondrian that set Calder on his path towards Mobiles, but the shapes that we now associate so much with his moving sculptures, were more inspired by his friend Miro. We should also note that Mondrian had a different attitude to chance in art. The year before Calder's visit to Mondrian, he wrote in his essay *Pure Abstract Art*: "But with such simple means it is difficult to achieve the deepest plastic expression: nothing can be left to accident; the most exact technique is required."[100]

The meeting between Mondrian and Calder in Mondrian's studio is in my opinion an overlooked tipping point in art history! Calder could have asked if he himself might be permitted to move those colored rectangles around. Or, Mondrian could have asked if Calder wanted to move around those rectangles in any way he felt like. But the fact is that neither of them suggested anything like that!

Had either of them done so, Participatory Art might have taken a huge stride forward. Instead, Mobile Art became a manifest form of art on a grand scale, thanks to Calder's special genius. Where Mondrian was aiming for art that *appeared* to move, Calder aimed at art that actually *did* move.

Calder was not particularly intellectually oriented, so the above exchange is all that Calder tells us about this visit. Thus, it seems we will never know if Mondrian also told Calder about his ideas of Neo-Plasticism and Open Form that he had been elaborating on for more than a decade.[101] Calder's Mobiles are in a sense very much about open form. But to Mondrian, the curved line – even in its most abstract form, the circle – was anathema. Clearly, Calder did not share this view. Maybe this explains Mondrian's reticence on the subject of Calder's mobiles.

From the point of view of Participatory Art, however, we must notice that perhaps the very genius of Calder – his inventiveness and his original thinking – put a limit on him. Not only did he develop the almost unlimited movement fully, for the first time in art history: *the endless variation, the open-ended work of art,* as a fundamental aspect of a work of art. Calder was also the first to introduce abstract *monumental* sculpture. (Tatlin appears to have been the first to develop abstract sculpture as such and several of the constructivists developed it further in the 1920s.) Arp called these huge, abstract sculptures of Calder's "stabiles" in 1932.

Given Calder's pioneering role, it is a bit unfair to fault Calder for not having developed his art in any other direction than he did. But with the wisdom of hindsight, it is hard not to see how well poised Calder was to "invent" also Participatory Art. More than any of his contemporary artists, *Calder* preserved a childlike quality of appreciating the importance and fun of play (cf. his *Circus*). He seemed to be totally free of prestige-seeking. He was no stranger to the spectator becoming involved in his Mobile Art by setting one of his mobiles in motion, by blowing air at it, or even giving it a gentle push ("mobils à main"). Calder seemed to approve of this kind of participation by the spectator.[102] In the 1998 Educational Broadcasting Corporation documentary on Calder, he himself can be seen blowing at one of his mobiles. This event looks to have been recorded sometime in the 1930-40s.[103]

From the point of view of Participatory Art, however, in Calder's mobiles the role of the spectator is still fundamentally passive. Very little scope has been given to the spectator's own *creative* powers to make any particular *choices* except the one of initiating a movement, the consequences of which can only be fairly uncontrolled by the initiator. Calder went from exploring mechanical movement in art to chance or random movement in art. But he stopped short of exploring human movement as expressed in human choice, and without choice you can neither explore creativity nor human responsibility and growth – so much needed in our times and in our future.

How come Calder developed in the direction of his stabiles rather than in the direction of Participatory Art? Part of the explanation may be that he was an engineer by training as well as a skilled craftsman, enjoying crafting things with his own two hands, as expressed in his many wire sculptures.

Henry Moore and form through divided units

Another interesting development within art, that perhaps eventually paved the way for Participatory Art, also took place in the 1930s. This was the decade when Henry Moore created his monumental sculptures, often in the shape of reclining women, in the form of separate volumes. Taken together, they made up a new sculpture, not a group of sculptures. From a Participatory Art point of view, Moore's reflections at the time about this new kind of sculpture are particularly relevant: "But it may now be no longer necessary to close down and restrict sculpture to the single (static) form unit. We can now begin to open out. *To relate and combine together several forms of varied sizes, sections, and directions into one organic whole.*"[104] (My italics.) From a Participatory Art point of view, Moore's comments here about his own kind of sculptures could equally well describe the fundamental principles of Participatory Art! Moore, of course, never took any further steps in the direction of opening up sculpture towards Participatory Art. He opened out sculpture, as he described it himself, but did not proceed to open out the traditional role of the artist as expert, the artist as "auteur", and the spectator as a passive onlooker. I doubt he was at all aware of or even interested in this as a problem. In all fairness, I must say that by doing what he did in sculpture, I think he already achieved more than enough for a lifetime.

Lázló Moholy-Nagy and the first deliberate Participatory Art work

Instead, the first time we know of, when an artist in a

deliberate way had the *participation* of the spectator in mind in creating the work of art and making it the main focus of at least one piece of art, was when Lázló Moholy-Nagy made his "transformable" Space Modulator L3, in 1936. Here, the spectator was invited (we have to presume) to move colored or black-and-white headed needles into any hole on a perforated background that was painted with two circles of different size. The larger circle contained three thin stripes of various lengths, positioned at an angle to the base line.[105] Elsewhere, similar pieces of art by Moholy-Nagy have been depicted as "paintings on sheets of cork, where some of the shapes are removable and fitted with needles on the back so that you can place them in different positions and in that way change the composition."[106]

By this time, Moholy-Nagy had served as a professor at both the first (1923-28) and the second Bauhaus. Perhaps it was no coincidence then that Moholy-Nagy was the one who made the first pieces of Participatory Art. In the early 1920s, both Johannes Itten and Filippo Tommaso Marinetti stressed that "*touch* had an intuitive, psychological value and role." (My italics.)[107] At the same time in Berlin, however, Moholy-Nagy had been deeply impressed by the sheer *creativity* of the Berlin Dadaists, their emphasis on *freedom* and the *role of chance*,[108] and "the idea of the artist not participating directly in the creation of his own work" (cf. Duchamp).[109] Moholy-Nagy, however, differed from them in his belief in "the liberation of man, the development of his creative abilities" being the purpose of art.[110] With his colleague from the Bauhaus, Joseph Albers, Moholy-Nagy shared "an interest in the outright eradication of the presence of the artist's hand in the making of the object.[111]

In issue no 4 of the magazine De Stijl 4, October 1921, Moholy-Nagy signed the "Manifesto on Elemental Art" (together with Raoul Hausmann, Hans Arp, Ivan Puni, among others). The manifesto, among other statements, declared:

> "We stand for elemental art. *Art* is elemental because it does not philosophize, because *it builds up its products from elements of its own* (my italics). To yield to the elements of creativity means to be an artist. *The elements of art cannot be determined by the artist alone.*"(My italics.)[112]

In 1922, in *Der Sturm,* Moholy-Nagy and Alfréd Kémeny published a kind of manifesto called *Dynamic-Constructive Forces,* where he and Kémeny stressed *Man's inherent creative power:*

> "We must therefore replace the *static* principle of classical art with *the dynamic principle of universal life.* Stated practically: instead of *static* material construction (material and form relations) dynamic construction (vital construction and *force relations*) must be evolved in which the material is employed only as *the carrier of forces.* Carrying further the unit of construction, A DYNAMIC-CONSTRUCTIVE SYSTEM OF FORCES is attained whereby *man, hitherto merely receptive* (my italics) in his observations of works of art, experiences a heightening of his own faculties, and *becomes himself an active partner* (my italics) with the forces unfolding

themselves.[113] (Italics except for the last two are from the original.)

Here are ideas that may have inspired Calder as well as Moore, but with a new role clearly envisaged for the spectator. It is intriguing that the authors of this Manifesto could spell out their interest in man becoming "an active partner," yet neither of them seem to have carried out their conviction in the shaping of their own art at that time. One cannot help wonder what prevented them from doing so. Not until 1935-36, did Moholy-Nagy create what looks to be the world's first deliberately created Participatory Art work. Perhaps it is no coincidence that Moholy-Nagy was the first to do it. Some 13 years earlier, he had stated the principles in the *Dynamic-Constructive Forces* manifesto quoted above. He had also explicitly spoken highly of Brancusi's sculptures as "a triumph of *relations* pure and simple". If Participatory Art is anything it is about relations and spectator creativity. Of some relevance is also that Moholy-Nagy had a keen interest in teaching and hence in the development of human beings.

From 1922 and onwards, Moholy-Nagy, inspired by Russian constructivists, created sculptures that can be seen as precursors to Op-Art. They contained a certain element of participation. Out of highly polished metal, glass, and wood, Moholy-Nagy created sculptures "in which the movement of the viewer reveals the first stage of a free play of light in space that is produced by the mirror like reflecting material."[114] Pointing in the same direction, Moholy-Nagy, between 1922-1930, worked on an early kind of Kinetic sculpture called the *Light Prop* or *Light Space-Modulator,* of which he also made a film.

In 1923, Moholy-Nagy became professor at Bauhaus in Germany.[115] In his first book, published in 1924, Moholy-Nagy expressed his belief that "the creative artist is one who recreates not art but life itself that is himself, in the spirit of the *Gesamtkunstwerk*"[116]. When Bauhaus dissolved, Moholy-Nagy moved first to London and then in 1937 to Chicago, forming a new design school for the Association of Arts and Industries. He called it the New Bauhaus and modeled it on the Dessau Bauhaus. In 1939 he opened his own school, the Chicago School of Design (since 1944 bearing its present name the Institute of Design and still considered one of the best design schools in the world). From a Participatory Art perspective, Moholy-Nagy's connections with Bauhaus were particularly important, carrying forward the belief of Bauhaus that everybody has talent, that is, trusting in the creative powers of ordinary people. However, Moholy-Nagy's cardboard pieces from the 1930s did not have any significant effect. Nothing more seems to have been heard about them and now they are believed to have disappeared altogether.

A peculiar aspect of Moholy-Nagys pioneering work in Participatory Art is that he himself never made much of it. In his 1932 work on pedagogy – *The New Vision* – he listed five stages of sculpture from static to kinetic (moving),[117] but clearly did not at this stage include participation. In his "testament" from 1944, *Abstract of an Artist,*[118] nothing like Participatory Art is mentioned. Nor did Participatory Art get into the curriculum at the Institute of Design, as far as we know.

It would be interesting to know why Moholy-Nagy did not pursue the idea of participation any further. He seemed to have all of the necessary ingredients within reach. It seems he did not fully realize the implications of it all. Throughout his life, Moholy-Nagy wanted to take art out into the world, the industrial world included: In 1944, he became art adviser to the Parker Pen Company.[119] He may have realized that there was no market for things like Participatory Art. Or, maybe, time was simply not right? A statement which Moholy-Nagy signed in October 1921, in the "Manifesto on Elemental Art", claims that "Art is the product of all the forces of an epoch;" and that "the artist is only an exponent of the forces which make manifest the elements of the world."[120] If this is true, how could he have taken Participatory Art any further than he did? Can art reflect something that is not yet in the times? Or, maybe, the upheavals of WW II plus personal problems became obstacles for Moholy-Nagy? He died of leukemia in 1946.

Participation, as such, did not play a major role in society until after WW II, when those who fought the war in the field and on the home front wanted a larger say in how to run the affairs of the country, after the war. Even so, participation was not very much in focus at the time. After Moholy-Nagy's experiments with Participatory Art in the latter part of the 1930s, a number of artists seem to have tinkered for a while with at least some works in the vein of Participatory Art. Basically, however, they were more or less just variations on either Mobile Art or Op Art, without a theory of their own. These artists include Gyula Kosice and Bruno Munari. However, it is only after the upheavals of WW II, at the now famous exhibition at Galerie Denise René in April 1955, that something akin to Participatory Art again surfaces in the history of art to any prominent extent.

Naum Gabo and Constructivism as a pre-theory of Participatory Art.

As we shall see in the next chapter Eco had read Gabo's writings prior to launching his concept Open Work around 1960. In his book from 1962, Eco quotes Gabo's letter to Herbert Read in 1944 summing up Constructivism.[121] Gabo and Pevsner represent a more idealist form of Constructivism and the Constructivism of the *Circle* in London, rather than the Russian, more materialist Constructivism of Tatlin, Rodchenko and the *Inkhuk* kind.[122] Gabo wrote: "We all construct the image of the world as we wish it to be, and this spiritual world of ours will always be what and how we make it. It is Mankind alone that is shaping it in a certain order out of a mass of incoherent and inimical realities. This is what it means to be Constructive." In the same letter, Gabo further elaborated on his thoughts about the shaping capacity of mankind. He did this in a way that clearly points in the direction of Eco's concept of the Open Work and even further towards the concept of Participatory Art, though he never used such a concept. In his letter to Herbert Read, Gabo also wrote that. ..."I have come to the conclusion that a work of art, restricted to what the artist has put in it, is only a part of itself. *It only attains full stature with what people and time make of it.*" (My italics.)

Speaking of his concept, the Constructive Idea, Gabo also wrote in the same letter: "It involves the whole complex of *human relation to life*. It is a mode of thinking, acting, perceiving and living. The Constructive philosophy recognizes only one stream in our existence – life (you may call it creation, it is the same). Any thing or action which enhances life, propels it and adds to it something in the direction of growth, expansion and development, is Constructive. The 'how' is of secondary importance". (My italics.) Then he adds: "Therefore to be constructive in art does not necessarily mean to be abstract at all costs."

Finally, speaking of the word 'perfection', which apparently Gabo had used on several previous occasions, he wrote: "I never meant 'perfection' in the sense of the superlative of good. 'Perfection', in the Constructivist sense, is not a state but a process; not an ultimate goal but a direction. *We cannot achieve perfection by stabilizing it – we can achieve it only by being in its stream*" (My italics).

In its practice, Constructivism was tied to the older forms of art by its relationship to the spectator being focused on contemplation.[123] Participatory Art, by contrast, relies on the practical, physical or near-physical, involvement of the spectator for its completion, for fully coming into being.

When Gabo wrote about the importance of creativity, he had in mind the creativity of the artist reaching its apex in the creative genius, not the creativity residing in the spectator, as in Participatory Art.

To Gabo, at least in 1937, the big problem of sculpture was how to incorporate and reconcile the traditional role of mass in sculpture with the new constructivist interest in the role of space and even time in sculpture. In sculpture of the Participatory Art-kind we find included also the dynamic element of process mirroring the increasing interest since WW II in dynamic systems, ecology being the prime example today.

Summing up the first half of the 20th century from the point of view of Participatory Art

During the first few decades of the 20th century, various radically new ideas kept popping up in art. At that time, the ideas were too few and too far between, and lacked enough cohesive articulation to gather the critical mass necessary to form a movement of their own. This is a way of saying that all those initiatives were ahead of their times when they first appeared. These radically new ideas – most of them emanating one way or another from Marcel Duchamp – may be summed up as appearing between 1910 and 1920. They are:

- a *transitional* concept of art
- a *new role for the spectator* in relation to the work of art was perceived beyond the traditional ones of payment and/or perception and contemplation
- some kind of *physical contribution from the spectator* was demanded which in turn led to *choice* and therefore possibly also to *responsibility*
- the *artist's personal control* of the final work of art was relinquished
- the *value of authorship* for the artist was put into question
- the role of *chance* was seen as a potentially fundamental contributing factor in the making

of a work of art

- - actual *physical movement* as part of the work of art became of greater interest
- the *creative process as such*, not just the results of creativity, was found important

In the 1920s to 1930s, these principles were basically encompassed, explored, experimented with and further developed by a few more artists, none of which stand out more than any other, from a Participatory Art point of view.

The 1930s saw less of a development from the point of view of Participatory Art. Few artists showed much interest. Nevertheless, three crucial developments did take place:

- - introduction on a large scale by Calder of *the open-ended work of art* where *endless variation* (within the framework of each work of art) was an integral part of the art work.
- - introduction of the *broken up sculpture*, that is, a work of art made up of separate pieces that did not function independently. By this I mean art made of two or more free-standing but *interdependent* pieces, depending on the relationship between them, to form the work of art as a whole, as in Moore's reclining figures. This arrangement is different from, for example, a group of human figures like Rhodin's *Burgers of Calais*.
- - introduction of the work of art, made from the outset *to involve the spectator's "creative powers"* as

an integral part of the work of art, as Moholy-Nagy tried to do.

All these ideas were later to become integral to Participatory Art.

PART III

HISTORICAL UNFOLDING IN THE 1950s AND 1960s

The 1950s and 1960s and the unfolding of Participatory Art

If we want to pinpoint a certain time and place for when and where Participatory Art started to unfold in earnest, I suggest we put that date to around 1950 and place it in Europe. In France it started as "L'Art Transformable" and in Germany as "Mitmachkunst." At this time, however, this kind of art did not become a school in the sense of having its own theories, principles, and dedicated followers, nor was it even a movement with a manifesto. It did not have a gallery promoting it exclusively, as Galerie Denise René promoted abstract art, Kinetic Art and Multiples from the end of the 1940s and onward. All this might account for the low recognition of Participatory Art up until present times. Another reason for this could be, of course, the very spectacular developments taking place in art in America during precisely these decades. For a long time, Abstract Expressionism, Pop Art, Minimalism and Conceptual Art, to a great extent overshadowed any other contemporary art.

A third and a more commercial reason could be that, because Participatory Art in principle is "un-signable", it does not appeal to the large-scale complex of galleries, collectors, museums, art fairs, auction rooms.[124] and hence will not gather the same publicity as big names and big sums of money. (In actual practice, however, though not out of necessity, Multiples were often connected to big names). Maybe the Participatory Art artists/practitioners will even in retrospect be seen more kindred to fairly anonymous change agents such as those who developed Wikipedia, rather than to the "artist-heroes" of bygone times. This would revert to more of a pre-renaissance role of the artist.

Yet, as this essay will show, Participatory Art does exist and has indeed existed for quite some time. But how can we understand the idea of Participatory Art? This essay is an effort to help people understand it by describing it from its unobtrusive, very rare and scattered beginnings at the roots of Modernism and in particular Dadaism, Constructivism, the Bauhaus and Kinetic Art, throughout the 20th century, up until today. On this journey we have now reached the years following after WW II.

It is worth remembering that the artists living through WW II had all, directly or indirectly, been witnessing human destructiveness on a scale hitherto impossible, indeed hitherto unimaginable; and for the second time in a generation at that! Trans-national peace-preaching movements, religion, and political ideologies founded on international solidarity, for example, socialism, had failed to prevent this disaster. Clearly, just reconstruction in itself, as after WW I, would not prevent destruction on this scale from re-occurring. This situation, I believe, left a vacuum of ideas beneficial for art to explore and to use, in trying to figure out what humanness is. And art explored these themes widely!

With the advantage of hindsight, we can see that the obvious excesses of human destructive capacity witnessed during the war led to shock, grief and dismay, and by and by also to a renewed interest in the opposite – in human constructive capacity, that is, in human *creativity*, as alsohappened after WW I. However, there is no evidence that this question was a central concern in the artistic circles of the time. From how art developed in the 10 years or so that followed WW II, we can only surmise that for a few artists at the time, how to free *the creativity of the spectator* became a legitimate and interesting question, even though marginally so, that fuelled various early efforts in the vein of Participatory Art.

Apart from the creativity of man, the *participation* of ordinary people also became an issue after WW II. During the war, the hidden capacities of ordinary people who had been called up to serve both in the forces and on the home front, had become highly visible (not least the capacities of women). The elites had to a large extent become discredited because of the war. A witness to that process was Churchill's loss to the Labor Party in the first postwar elections in Great Britain. More people wanted more of a say, and they wanted to construct something new and better, rather than just reconstruct the old that had failed so dismally; just as was the case after the great upheavals in France around the middle of the 19th century, leading on to various isms culminating in Cubism and a totally different way of looking at art. After the catastrophe of WWI, generating or fuelling Dadaism and abstract art, the process repeated itself after WWII. Now the new was once again perceived as having an intrinsic value. The fact that some key artists of the post WW I era were now gone may also have been a contributing factor. In 1944 alone, Kandinsky, Moholy-Nagy and Mondrian all died – three highly influential art theorists as well as artists.

The early and mid 1950s saw something of a revival of Dadaism, perhaps chiefly recognizable in the Fluxus-movement. A trend involving among others Jasper Johns, Robert Rauschenberg and the musician John Cage were even "fleetingly called Neo-Dada"[125]. There was also a revival of Kinetic art. On the whole, the 1950s and 1960s saw an almost explosive development in art that lasted well into the 1990s, especially in the United States. In Europe at the same time, however, a much less recognized tendency built up momentum. Gradually, and without forming a movement, a number of artists began exploring the theme of *active spectator participation* in various forms, but usually only as a small part of their artistic work, never as the main focus of their work. Contributing to this renaissance of something in the vein of Participatory Art were two other developments within art at this time.

At the beginning of the Modern Movement, Marcel Duchamp and Man Ray had put into question the paramount value of the unique work of art, of the "original" work of art, for the communication of the artist's ideas and intentions. In fact, with Duchamp's

Ready-mades, the whole idea of the uniqueness of a work of art being essential to the concept of art disappeared. This *disappearance of the unique work being central to the concept of art* obviously also paved the way for *art made in series without any one item being the original work of art*, as in industrial production. For some artists, as we will see below when we discuss Multi Art, this seemed to make possible an art for the masses, art that could be afforded even by people other than those going to galleries and museums. This marriage of art and the industrial production and distribution processes had also been a dream of some artists after WW I.

Out of Kinetic Art, for example, the mobiles of Calder, and perhaps also out of the writings of Mondrian, the notion of *the open-ended work of art* was further developed. This diminished the importance of the unique art object, as the varieties could be infinite. Instead, the logical consequence would be to make series of each work of art and seek as wide a distribution as possible. This led on to what eventually became called Multi Art.

Denise René and the highly important *Mouvement*-exhibition in 1955

In November 1944, Denise René opened the now famous Galerie Denis René in central Paris, at the suggestion of her friend Victor Vasarely. The intention was to create a rallying point for some of the new artists interested in the role of a new art in the construction of a new society. The gallery would also act as a bridge between the pre WW II avant-garde and postwar art. Denise René played her bridging role by exhibiting early modernist abstract/constructivist art together with new art. By bringing the older artists together with a younger generation, René created a continuation of thought as well as a stimulus for new thinking, especially in the direction of *abstract art*. The Galerie Denis René with its associated artists functioned much like the hub and spokes in a wheel of innovations in European art after WW II.

In 1955, Galerie Denise René launched the milestone exhibition *Mouvement* which resulted in a breakthrough for both Kinetic Art (pioneered by Gabo and Pevsner in 1920) and Op Art (or optical art).[126] The latter was described by René as leaving behind the classical rules of composition and color, in an effort to express *motion* (unlike the futurists some 50 years earlier), while respecting the picture plane and without seeking recourse in elements outside the picture.[127] Some of the artists at this exhibition would also work with Multiples.

The *Mouvement* exhibition was a turning point for Galerie Denise René and for abstract art in general and in particular for Mobile Art and Op Art (and for Participatory Art, but this has never been fully acknowledged, as far as I know). This exhibition inspired the 1961 exhibition "Rörelse i Konsten" at Moderna Museet (The Modern Museum) in Stockholm, Sweden and at Staedelijk in Amsterdam, The Netherlands, and to some extent also the 1967 exhibition *Lumiére et Mouvement* in Paris. Among those who showed some works in 1955 were Vasarely, Agam, Jacobsen, Bury, Soto and Tinguely. Alexander Calder and Marcel Duchamp were represented at the exhibition as a bridge to the pre WW II artistic Avant Garde.

Victor Vasarely was the first artist to exhibit at Galerie Denise René. Vasarely came to Paris in 1931 to work as a graphic designer. His training came from having attended the Mühely Art Academy in Budapest, Hungary, which was modeled on The Bauhaus School in Dessau, Germany.[128] More than anyone before him, Vasarely explored optical phenomena on one plane that gave the spectator the sensation of movement, to begin with only in black and white. I see this as a continuation of Duchamp's "invention" of Op Art with *Rotary Glass Plaques/Revolving Glass* (1920) and *Rotary Demispere* (1925) as well as *Gabo's* work in the 1920s. In a sense Vasarely's art was also a continuation of the ambiguous pictures of late 19th early 20th century.

Though primarily oriented towards Kinetics at the perceptual level, Vasarely also experimented with the concept of "ideomotoric movement". This concept represents an experience independent of moving parts but dependent on spectator movement. Here, the aim is not to create the sensation of movement but making movement a prerequisite for fully experiencing the work of art. To some extent this is, of course, true for all forms of sculpture. The first artists to use it as an integral part of the work of art was perhaps Duchamp in his large work on transparent glass (*"La Mariée..."*). Moholy-Nagy experimented in the 1920s with the changing patterns formed by sheets of cut out metal, placed in front of one another as the spectator moved in front of these objects.[129] He also worked with shadows from sculptures being projected onto walls and with pieces of transparent material on different planes. The tradition goes back at least to Adolph Appia and his *Music and the Stage Setting* from 1895.[130] The first artist to give a theoretical underpinning to the spectators' movement as central to the work of art, seems to have been Katarzyna Kobro, during the latter part of the 1920s[131].

On a small scale Vasarely also experimented with combining "ideomotoric movement" and Participatory Art (without using that term). One example is a set of small, square, interchangeable transparencies, each with a certain pattern printed on it (not unlike what Moholy-Nagy had pioneered in the 1939s), leaving the spectator to combine and recombine them, resulting in new patterns and effects.[132]

The impetus to "ideomotoric movement" may have originated from the *Lincoln-Wilson method*, where creases in a surface can be exploited by the artist in order to *paint several pictures in one*. It could only be discovered by the spectator if he or she moved. But was this really so different from the changing impressions emerging when spectators walked around, say, a Giacometti sculpture? Connoisseurs of sculpture had always known the importance of seeing the sculpture from all angles. "Sculpture fully in the round has no two points of view alike." wrote Henry Moore in 1934.[133]

Yakoov Agam had been trained by Johannes Itten after Itten left Bauhaus.[134] His art is of particular interest from the point of view of Participatory Art. Through what was called *Transformables*, Agam seems to have been the first artist after Moholy-Nagy to explore the integration of movement with art, and of the special movement consisting of the physical involvement of the spectator in actually physically changing an exhibited work of art in endless or smaller number of variations, albeit still within a pre-set framework. From the point of view of

Participatory Art, Agam often limited the creativity of the spectator, however. In a sense Agam was still using the spectator as a motor in fairly open-ended works of art. In any event, the creativity of the spectator was never the main focus of his art. In the Artist's Credo at the end of a book about Agam, in 1980, Agam emphasizes that "the key to my work is the attempt to give plastic definition to the concept of Hebrew realism beyond the limits of religion and to open the gateway which leads to reality." At the very beginning of his Credo he also states that "All the aspects of my work – painting, sculpture, graphics, and so on – may be related to the experience of one man, one individual: that is, the artist himself." This is clearly at odds with the main interests of Participatory Art, which is the creativity of others and the creative moment as such. In fact, in this Credo of Agam's he does not mention the role of the spectator, the creative moment, or the creativity of the spectator.[135]

In particular, Vasarely, Agam as well as Soto, all three belonging to the group around Galerie Denis René in Paris, explored Optical Art. Agam and Soto often used different levels of plexiglas, creating a changing picture for the spectator as the spectator moved in front of the picture ("ideomotoric movement" from the movement in art point of view[136]). As mentioned above, this was an effect or a technique pioneered by Duchamp in his extensive work on transparent glass (*"La Mariée..."*) and by Moholy-Nagy in the 1930s (his *Space Modulators* series[137]).[138] But never before had artists focused on this technique to such an extent as was done at the *Mouvement* exhibition and, particularly by Soto, for several years afterwards.

As late as in the 1960s, the act of moving around in relation to a work of art played a central role in a new kind of art, Minimalism. "For it is the viewer who changes the shape constantly by his change in position relative to the work" wrote Robert Morris in 1966. "A Baroque figurative bronze is different from every side. So is a six-foot cube. The constant shape of the cube held in the mind but which the viewer never literally experiences, is an actuality against which the literal changing, perspective views are related. There are two distinct terms: the known constant and the experienced variable. Such a division does not occur in the experience of the bronze."[139] The question is, how much actual participation from the spectator does this invite, and how interesting an experience is this in itself? We may also ask whether it is more of a perceptual/psychological experience than an aesthetic experience, such as walking around the Baroque bronze might be.

The Venezuelan artist Jesus-Rafael Soto created among other artworks a blend of Kinetic Art and Op-Art, making optical reliefs, or using thin rods and plates of metal suspended in front of horizontal lines made up of strings. He then went on to create what he called "le penetrable" – a penetrable kind of installation. In the latter, the spectator is invited to enter a mass of "vertical lines" hanging from the ceiling. But *the creativity of the spectator, as a basis for creating the final work of art,* was not a major concern of any of the artists at Galerie Denise René.

Jean Tinguely emphasized the mechanically driven movement, but like those who used motors in art before him - for example Duchamp, Gabo, Calder, Moholy-Nagy, and Mortensen (in his huge 1944 mechanical painting) – he left very little room for the spectators' involvement, save pressing a button. Tinguely's crank-operated sculptures (like those of his predecessor Heinrich Anton Müller in the mental hospital in Bern) really only *left the spectator to decide the speed of the movement.*

The Danish sculptor Robert Jacobsen was another artist in the early circle around the Galerie Denis René. At the time, he was living in Paris, focusing on creating movement *within* a sculpture, that is, movement without any moving parts and little, if any, participation from the spectator, except the ideomotoric movement. Alongside these kinds of sculptures, however, Jacobsen also made dolls out of metal scrap. To begin with, he made them as toys for his little daughter, but he was hardly unaware that they might be regarded as sculptures to be handled by the spectator. Perhaps these dolls were regarded even more as sculptures than the dolls of Hannah Höch and Sophie Taeuber-Arp in 1916 and 1918 respectively, or the figures in Calder's *Circus* of 1926-1930.

Yet another artist who experimented with a blend of Kinetic Art, light reflections and elementary participation by the spectators was the Hungarian-born Nicolas Schöffer. He began adding movement to his "spatiodynamic" sculptures already in 1948. In 1956, he constructed a sculpture which responded to light and sound.[140]

At the Documenta 4 in 1968, at least one artist exhibited something with a Participatory Art orientation – Kenneth Martin (1905-1984). Martin was a British artist who, together with Mary Martin and Victor Pasmore, had been part of the constructivist revival in Britain and America toward the end of the 1940s. Judging from the entries in the exhibition catalogue it is difficult to tell how many of the 12 pieces in Martin's exhibition represented something in the vein of Participatory Art. Names like "Transformable", "Screw mobile" and "Rotary Rings" suggested that some of them were. "Transformable" and "Rotary Rings" are displayed in photographs in the catalogue. The spectator's freedom to use his/her creativity seems more on the level of Agam than of some later artists.

Hans Haacke's "audience participatory installation"[141] called *Documenta Visitors' Profil* exhibited at the Documenta V in 1972, might serve as an example of both how these trends continued into the 70s and how various artists made just one or a few pieces in the vein of Participatory Art, but no well known artist stuck exclusively to this kind of art for the whole of their careers.

The exhibitions of Mobile Art in 1961 at Moderna Museet in Stockholm (Rörelse i konsten) and at Stedelijk in Amsterdam, had the potential of being for Participatory Art of the 1960s what the Galerie Denis René had been for Kinetic art and Op Art in the 1950s. Far from being the central focus of the exhibition, however, (the concept Participatory Art did not exist before 1982, as far as I know), at least those exhibitions allowed various participatory aspects in art to be seen and discussed on par with other trends in contemporary art. This did not, however, result in much documentation of such discussions and even less in a new kind of art becoming established. In most cases spectator involvement was presented only as an amusing variety of Mobile Art, some times just as a fun thing done by a well-known artist, rather than an independent kind of art. One reason for this may be that no well-established artist was focusing and/or driving the development of Participatory Art as such. So far, to my knowledge no well known artist has dedicated him or herself exclusively to field of Participatory Art. Even less did there exist a theory behind it.

Multi Art entwined with Participatory Art

Multiples began as an early offshoot of the exhibition at Galerie Denise René. In 1959-1960, Daniel Spoerri made an effort at mass distribution of art by gathering a number of artists creating Multiples and marketing them under the name *Edition MAT 1959/60*. The name MAT stood for Multiplication d'Art Transformable. As the name implies there was a clear ambition to involve the spectator to a greater or lesser extent, an ambition that disappeared with later editions (the last one being in 1965, but not under Daniel Spoerri's aegis). New venues for art were explored by, for example, Danese Edizioni (1959), selling, among others, *Travelling Sculpture* (made of blue cardboard in an edition of 1000[142]) by Bruno Munari through furniture shops.

Multi Art, or multiples for short, very much a phenomenon of the 1950s and 1960s, may not at first sight seem to have much in common with Participatory Art. Yet, there are some important connections, not only through names such as Duchamp and Beuys, but more so in the philosophy behind both kinds of art.

The Modern Movement – especially early on through Duchamp and Ray – had put into question the paramount value of *the unique work of art*, the original, in the communication of the artist's conception or idea. With Duchamp's *Readymades* and his *Boites-en-valise*, for example, the whole idea of a unique work, as a necessity for art, disappeared. Kinetic Art or mobiles could be seen as *open-ended works of art*. A logical consequence was to ensure that what was created was given the widest possible distribution. This in turn pointed the way toward mass-fabricated and hence far less expensive art.

Multi Art had an ideological aspect in the sense that some artists saw it as a way to put art within reach of the masses and not just of wealthy collectors. This could be done by making series of art works without any one being "the original", or the first in a series being better than the last. Thus there would be no reproductions of an original. Mostly, very simple production techniques suited to industrial production were used. The French painter Jean Fautrier had experimented with different ways of making pictures as "originaux multiples" – non-unique paintings – already back in 1949 and until 1954[143].

In 1959-1960, Daniel Spoerri through his venture Edition MAT arranged a series of exhibitions in various European cities including Paris, Zurich and Stockholm. On show were works of art that, rather than being unique, were made in series of sometimes several hundred copies each. This was the logical conclusion of much abstract art, including Kinetic Art. They were not carrying a personal imprint like brushwork does. Kinetic Art, almost by definition, was itself variable and sometimes endlessly so, like Calder's mobiles.

In this first Edition MAT, the connection to Participatory

Art was explicit (though that concept was not yet in use) as this first edition was devoted entirely to the "Multiplication d'Art Transformable" (MAT). Each piece of Multi Art in this collection could be "transformed" by the spectator, usually by the spectator moving (as in Op Art) or setting things in motion (as in Kinetic Art). Note however, that emphasis here was on *change* and *movement,* just as it had been at the Galerie Denis René exhibition in 1955. The list of those who took part[144] gives us a hint: It seems to have been the "nonstatic-ness" of a work of art in combination with the multiplication of each object – thereby doubly spiting the traditional art market – that was of major interest, rather than the creativity of the spectator and the challenge of involving that creativity in an interesting way.

Artists tried out new venues for art. Danese Edizioni, for example, tried to sell through shops for modern interior design. An interesting question, but a difficult one to answer, is, why did these efforts to spread art to the many never catch on? The reason cannot be found solely in the trends of the trade or the art market or in the behavior of consumers/spectators. Multi Art seems to have lacked an appeal to the artists themselves. One trend in American minimalist sculpture around 1968 reacted to the reduction of art into tradable goods by making site specific sculptures, often of monumental proportions.[145]

Multiples had its heydays in the 1960s. Early retrospectives emerged already in the 1970s, leading to a decline in the late 1970s and to a second golden age in the late 1980s, this time in other forms.[146]

To Participatory Art, with its inherent focus on the

creativity of the spectator and not solely in the creativity of the artist, the mass production aspect is not a problem, save for the risk of overexposure of one "kit", if you like. As each "kit" often contains an almost endless amount of possibilities, this kind of art actually needs a wide distribution for the work of art to become fully manifest.

Even though there is no absolute connection between Multiples and Participatory Art, there is a logical connection in the lack of interest in the intrinsic value of the unique object. As a Participatory Art work by definition can take many shapes and forms, why limit it to one art work? Doing so would only limit the number of people whose creativity can be involved and enhanced. What could possibly be gained – except increased commercial value due to short supply – by creating unique pieces of Participatory Art? Producing limited, though large, editions could save a piece of art from over-exposure. But would that be a risk with Participatory Art, which is open-ended and builds on diversity? On the other hand - would we feel comfortable if Calder's mobiles had been produced in endless series?

Multiples and Participatory Art also share similar goals in that both are aimed at bringing art outside the narrow circle of galleries, collectors and museums.

Comparisons between Multi Art and Participatory Art may include:

-   both seek to expand the concept of art.
-   both seek to free art from getting reduced to a commercial item. The means to free art is by

freeing art objects from the idea of the special value of the unique object.

- Both seek to free the artist from the constraints of the art market.

- Both seek to bring art down from the pedestal it has increasingly been placed upon during the last 100 years, though they do this in different ways. Participatory Art encourages art beyond the pedestal, in reaching the many, or more specifically, the creativity of the many, rather than becoming yet another possession for the many as would Multi Art. Mass-producing art in a semi-industrial manner would be one way to do this.

Out of the same scene that brought us the Multiples, seems to have come also a few early experiments with something in the vein of Participatory Art. But just as no artist became known only by creating multiples, no artist at that time focused singularly on creating something in the vein of Participatory Art.

Destruction as participation

In the late 1950s, Mobile Art reached its ultimate frontier, when it merged with *happenings* in the *auto-destructive artwork*. Gustav Metzger (born 1926) wrote his manifesto of auto-destructive art in 1959, stating that "work should be derived from the real world, be machine-made and temporary, and undergo a transformation over a period of time."[147] In 1966, Metzger organized the now famous DIAS (Destruction in Art Symposium). In the meantime, Metzger had written his third manifesto in 1961 where he introduced the converse kind of art. Auto-creative art was an "'art of change, movement and growth', where destruction remained an element of the work, but was a pre-condition of renewal and creation"[148] (cf. his *Liquid Crystals* consisting of light projections through chemicals in a perpetual flux).

The ideal here was the absence of human intervention rather than an increased presence. Metzger was more interested in speaking up as a witness against the destructive forces around him and against the art market, than he was in the creativity of the individual. Some of his works have been more of an interactive kind (*To Crawl Into, Vienna, March 1938*), some more a form of installation. Metzger focused on "the complexity of human experience, our effect on the natural world and how we live together"[149] rather than on the creativity of the individual.

With his *Homage to New York* in 1960, Jean Tingely constructed a combination of happening and a machine pre-programmed to destroy itself at a spectacular event at the MOMA. Auto-destructive art represents perhaps the very opposite of Participatory Art.

Eco's concept of the "open work"- a pre-theory of Participatory Art.

Towards the end of the 1950s Umberto Eco wrote a series of essays where he explored the role of "openness" in modern art. By "open work" he meant a work of art that deliberately, albeit to a greater or lesser extent, remains open to the reactions of the reader, listener or viewer for its full realization. The essays were published in Italian in 1962 under the name of "Opera Aperta" (Open Work) which later turned out to be a seminal concept in itself. The first English translation appeared only in 1989.[150]

It is difficult to estimate how much Eco's work influenced art at that time or if it was primarily a distillation of ideas already manifest in art. I suspect the latter to be the case. In any case, no one before Eco had made such an effort to construct a theory of the Open Work. Hence a few thoughts about this concept are included here.

The roots of the Open Work go back, according to Eco, to the late 19th century Symbolist movement. From another point of view the concept of Open Work might be regarded as a sub-category of Gille Dorfles' concept Informal Art – "a form of abstract art without any will to figurate and with no semantic intention" in the words of Eco. Eco did not use the concept Participatory Art, possibly because this concept did not exist in 1962, but as it could be regarded as a subcategory of "Open Work", it may be fruitful at this point to look further into Eco's deliberations on the "Open Work".

The concept of Open Work is clearly a wider concept than Participatory Art, but encompasses Participatory Art. Eco's ambition was neither to write about Participatory Art nor about the creativity of the spectator and how to build a work of art based on that creativity. The reason for Eco to propose the notion of Open Work was that it seemed particularly effective in explaining "some phenomena of contemporary art from the point of view of the intentions (poetics) underlying the artistic procedure, and of the historical reasons informing these intentions." Especially, Eco asked questions such as: "What notions of art motivate most of today's artists? To what extent does this new idea reflect the development of a modern aesthetic consciousness? And how do these intentions become methods of procedure, and, therefore, formal structures?" It seems obvious that Eco's focus was on the work of art as such and how it came about and not on the other aspect of the open work – what went on in the mind of the spectator or the degree of spectator involvement.

Characteristic for the Open Work is that it remains *unfinished* without an intervention of some kind by the spectator/listener/reader/performer/consumer. To some extent all art has, of course, been open to many different readings. Eco connected back to the freedom inherent in the dynamism of Baroque sculpture, that for the first time gave man a chance to opt out of "the canon of authorized responses"(like allegorical interpretations) and instead gave the spectator the chance to enjoy the work of art from any angle. More specifically, however, Eco mentioned the ambiguity and indeterminacy of the Symbolist movement as the beginning of the Open Work. Eco also put it this way: "The open work assumes the task of giving us *an image of discontinuity*. It does not narrate. It *is* it." …"allows us to *comprehend new aspects of the world*." The very basis of the concept Open Work is, as Eco called it, "an oriented production of open possibilities, of an incitement to experience *choice*" (My italics).

One of these new aspects of the world is the great role that *chance* plays in our lives. "In order to turn this chance into a cluster of possibilities, it is first necessary to provide it with some organization" and to formulate "a new grammar that rests not on a system of organization but on the assumption of disorder." The traditional narrative convention in art has automatically masked the "true fragmentary, dissociated nature" of any situation we may find ourselves in, according to Eco.

Eco's work covers all the arts and begins by noting how composers such as Stockhausen (*Klavierstück XI*), Berio (*Sequence*), Pousseur (*Mobiles* and *Scambi*) and Boulez (*Third Sonata for Piano*, first section) had created works that left part of the actual composing process for the listener to execute. Eco quotes Posseur saying that his piece *Scambi* was "not so much a musical composition as *a field of possibilities*, an explicit invitation to exercise choice."

In literature, Eco mentions that the Symbolist poet Mallarmé's only sketchily realized *Le livre* (he worked on it during the last three decades of the 19th century). He notes Kafka's entire oeuvre, Joyce's work, in particular *Finnegan's Wake* (1939), and the open end of many of Brecht's plays. Though Eco does not mention it, from a writer's point of view, any written play surely to some extent must be an open work – open to a limited group of people, as it depends for its full realization on the interpretation of both actors and the director. But from a spectator point of view, how much of a play is really the author's?

When he examines the pictorial and plastic arts, Eco mentions Duchamp and Calder as early examples of artist doing open work. As contemporary (end of the 1950s) examples he mentions (but only in a footnote): "Besides Munari's famous *vetrini*, one might also consider some experiments of the last generation: for example, the *Miriorama*" of the Group T (Aneschi, Boriani, Colombo, Devicchi), Yaacov Agams's transformable structures, Pol Bury's 'mobile constellations', Duchamp's *rotoreliefs* ('the artist is not alone in accomplishing his act of creation, since the spectator is the one who puts the work in contact with the exterior world by deciphering and interpreting its profound qualities, and thus he contributes to the creative process'), Enzo Mari's transformable objects, Munari's articulated structures, Dieter Rot's mobile sheets, Jesus Soto's Kinetic Structures ('These structures are kinetic because they use the spectator as motor. They reflect the movement of the spectator as well as that of his eyes. They foresee his capacity to move and solicit his activity without constraining it. They are Kinetic structures because they do not contain the forces that animate them, they borrow their dynamism from the spectator,' as Claus Bremer notes). Jean Tinguely's machines (which maneuvered by the spectator, keep drawing different configurations) and Vasarely's forms."[151]

In order to deem a work of art to be an Open Work, Eco used the criteria that the work should be "*brought to their conclusion by the performer*" (how this is done was of no interest to him, however). The work of art should be "*literally 'unfinished*'" and "*encourage 'acts of freedom'*." And thus the work consists of "*a network of limitless interrelations*." Other criteria are infinite possibilities, collaboration in the making. Or, in the case of Calder and Boulez "*consist of unplanned or incomplete structural units*." It seems crucial that *the artist is "giving up the essential focus of the composition and the prescribed point of view for its viewer*".

Eco quotes the composer Pousseur who talked about *"fields of possibilities"* and *"a configuration of possible events, a complete dynamism of structure."* Posseur had borrowed the concepts of field and possibilities from the contemporary canon in science and notably physics, with a *"devolution of intellectual authority to personal decision, choice and social context,"* as Eco put it.

At one point, Eco tried out the concept of "work in movement" and described this as "The possibility of numerous different personal interventions, but is not an amorphous invitation to *indiscriminate participation* (one of only a couple of times he uses the word participation, my comment). The invitation offers the performer the opportunity for an oriented insertion into something which always remains the world intended by the author." (My italics) "In other words, the author offers the interpreter, the performer, the addressee a work *to be completed.* He does not know the exact fashion in which his work will be concluded, but he is aware that once completed the work in question will still be his own". Presumably, it is this last distinction that differentiates Participatory Art from ordinary collaboration and co-creation in general. An encyclopedia is not a "work" in the same way an open work can be said to be.

At another point, Eco said that whereas the "aim of structural thought is to *discover"* ... *"that of serial thought is to produce".* Participatory Art, I would say, is about both discovering and producing. It is about discovering the complex nature of the creative moment and discovering your relationship to your own creativity; and doing this while you are producing something of no other use than the fact that it appeals to you aesthetically, in the widest sense including for instance experiencing your own vitality.

From all this we can see that Eco's concept of Open Work was indifferent to both the degree and the kind of involvement of the spectator's creativity. To Eco all levels of spectator involvement seemed to be just as much Open Work. Eco did not differentiate between levels or degrees of openness in any Open Work. This seems to be both a logical and rather instructive thing to do, however. I therefore suggest the following eight levels of openness, differentiated by the degree of spectator involvement for the work of art to come into being:

1. Works of open art that stress the role of chance in the coming into being of the work of art. Little or no concrete participation by the spectator in order to achieve completion.

Examples of such art might be the collages of Jean Arp, where fragments of colored paper were falling down onto a light background (1916-17). Carl Andre, when he emptied some white plastic "bricks" onto a gallery floor (1966). Richard Serra's object of molten lead called *Splashing* (1968).

2. Works of art that for their completion must be set in motion by the artist or someone else. The effect is independent of the person who sets it in motion, because once set in motion the work of art follows a preprogrammed pattern of movement.

Examples of this might be Duchamp's *Rotary Glass Plates* (1920). Possibly even *Bicycle Wheel* from 1913.

Rodchenko, Gabo and Moholy-Nagy during the 1920s. And then later Mortensen and Tinguely amongst others.

3. Works that need to be set in motion by someone or by the moving air or something similar and will then be moving but in a haphazard way. The role of the participating spectator could here be in choosing either the right moment or the right energy with which to start the movement, or both. Both choices will determine what the work of art does.

Examples: *Abat-Jour* by Man Ray (1920), possibly also some of the Kinetic art in the early 1920s and then Calder's mobiles.

4. Works of art that are executed by the spectator but according to fairly detailed instructions by the artist who may or may not be present at the execution. The limitation here lies in the detail of the instructions which will be limiting the choice and hence also the creativity of the spectator but nevertheless convey the feeling of creating.

Examples: Sol LeWitt's wall drawings from around 1970.

5. Works of art that depend on how you read them.

Example: Pictures based on ambiguity and pictures based on indeterminacy. Possibly also Duchamp's *"The Bride..."* and some of the Op-Art. Possibly also Conceptual Art.

6. Play-art. Toys designed by artists or works of art designed to be played with.

Examples: The dolls of Hannah Höchs (1916) and Sophie Taeuber Arp (1920), *"Dandanah". The Fairy Place"* by Bruno Taut from 1919-1927/28. Calder's *Circus* (1920s). A more recent example would perhaps be Olafur Eliasson exhibiting white Lego bricks for the spectator to build with.

7. Works of art that are incomplete unless the spectator "enters" the work or in any other way gets practically involved in it. Often this is done by physically entering the work of art. This might be described as participatory installations.

Examples: The first Dadaist exhibition in Cologne 1920. Schwitters' *Merzbau* (1919-1937). Oiticica's *Tropicália (1966)*. Some relational art from the 1980s onwards. Gormley's fogged up room in his South Bank Exhibition (2007).

8. Works of art already from the beginning made up of parts and which need the spectator's physical intervention, creativity and individual choices in order for the work of art to reach its completion. Yet, in one sense, never reaching and end state.

Examples: Moholy-Nagy in the 1930s, Agam in the 1950s, Lygia Clark, Charlotte Posenenske and Öyvind Fahlström in the 1960s, Participatory Art.

Lygia Clark – the escape from the art market and the exploration of participation

Just as it is impossible to write about the development of Participatory Art without mentioning Agam it is equally impossible to avoid mentioning the less known but more experimentally inclined Lygia Clark. As she spent a year in Paris studying painting for Leger in 1950-1951 it is possible that she and Agam knew about each other's work, but I have not found evidence of that. Clark's more direct source of stylistic inspiration, was the Swiss "Concrete Art" artist and former Bauhaus teacher Max Bill.

In number of actual works of art, Agam and Clark are poles apart. Agam was extremely prolific and market-oriented, and his works of art remained within the framework of collectible or tradable aesthetic objects, even though many of them invited some kind of spectator participation. In contrast, the works of Clark that invite spectator participation are actually quite few, perhaps just around a dozen, though *relational* and *reciprocity* seemed to be central values to her throughout her career. But "because her work does not fit within the institutional framework and the rather conventional notion of 'the work of art'"[152] her work is rarely seen. The room with some of her experimental propositions at the Documenta X, a presentation of her later works at Musée des Beaux Art in Nantes and 13 of her early works in an exhibition of the Rio Neoconcreto movement 1956-1964 at the Moderna Muséet in Stockholm 2008,[153] are later exceptions.

According to art critic Guy Brett, the evolution of Clark's work "may perhaps be summed up as a radical journey beyond the traditional relationship between artist and spectator".[154]

Lygia Clark was born in Brazil in 1920 and became an artist in 1947 doing monochrome paintings/reliefs followed by neo-constructivist work. She was a co-founder of the

Brazilian Neo-Constructivist movement (1959-64). She studied with Léger and Arpad Szenes in Paris 1950-52. In 1957, she took part in Rio de Janeiro's first National Concrete Art Exhibition. I mention these details because the rapid moves in her career, often combined with a crisis, was characteristic for Clark. Her crises were one reason for the relatively small volume of work. Some of the earliest works of a participatory character was Clark's short series *Bicho* (around 1960-1964). Fundamentally, these art objects were aluminum surfaces held together by hinges. The angles of the surfaces were thus alterable by the spectator and to some extent the total shape could thus also be altered. But the surfaces were not separable, thus limiting spectator choice. Clark described her work in these terms: "The Animal (Bicho) has his own and well-defined cluster of movements which react to the prompting of the spectator. He is not made of isolated functional forms which can be manipulated at random as in a game: no, his parts are functionally related to each other, as if he were a living organism."[155] From the early 1960s, Clark's works developed further in the direction of spectator participation. In a rather well formulated phrase, Suely Rolnik, art critic, curator and psychoanalyst, states that "...after 1963, the work could no longer exist anywhere but in the receiver's experience..."[156] And to some extent that could be said to be a characteristic of all Participatory Art. From this kind of art, she moved on, however, to sculptures that were more completely "open" or undefined, like *Borrachas* in 1964, and more action-oriented like the spectator/participant cutting along a Mobius loop in *Caminhando* and the choices involved in the cutting being the art work. The art work thus only lasted as long as the action went on and with scant if any aesthetic ambitions. Would this be different from a pedagogical tool?

In 1972 began the second of three major phases in Clark's career. During the years 1972-1976, Clark taught art at Sorbonne as part of deliberately moving away from the institutions of the art system. Her art at this time shifted toward creating multi-sensory experiences (*Collective Bodies*) for and with her students (deliberately not the usual art public). Through physical participation and by using "equipment" designed by Clark, her students, or participants as they were called, became active participants in various co-creative events on the level of individuals and groups. Clark's *Baba antropofágica* (1973) is an example. In a Frieze article in 2006, art critic Vivian Rehberg described Baba and other works from this phase as "communal psycho-sensorial experiments".[157] Had Clark by now left the realm of art?

The third phase of Clark's career began in 1979 after her final return in 1976 to Rio de Janeiro and lasted until her death from a heart attack in 1988. During this phase she had distanced herself almost completely from the dictums of the art market, art museums etcetera and moved her art into the realm of psychotherapy/healing. "By means of the Relational Objects, she believed an interaction was possible with experiences locked in the body's memory, at a nonverbal, or preverbal, level" according to art critic Guy Brett.[158] According to Suely Rolnik, Clark then focused on "the memory of trauma and of its fantasies/ phantoms, whose mobilization would now cease to a mere side-effect of the proposals and come instead to occupy the very nerve center of her new device."[159] Not so surprisingly, this ambition drove Clark into having psychotherapeutic ambitions with her work, recreating them so to speak with "receivers"(Rolnik's term) in hourly sessions. It seems the participation here also involved the projections of the clients. To Brett, this did not imply a change of métier but rather a transformation of the notions of art and of the artist as Clark "did not borrow existing concepts of art, or of representation, for use in a therapeutic context."[160]

Throughout these phases, Clark produced different kinds of interactive art. However, the creative moment or the creativity of the spectator/participant was never her main focus. According to Suely Rolnik, Clark's focus lay rather on the institutional critique typical for the 1960s and 1970s. Her objective was not primarily to address the creativity of the "spectator" but to achieve "multisensorial experiences, whose importance lies in overcoming the reduction of artistic research to the field of gaze. However, if on the one hand the exploration of the sense organs was an issue at the time, shared in fact by Clark, still the artist's work went further: the focus of her investigation consisted in mobilizing the two capacities inherent in each of the senses. I refer to the capacities of perception and sensation that allows us to apprehend the otherness of the world, respectively as a map of forms on which we project representations, or as a diagram of forces that affect all the senses in their capacity for resonance."[161]. From Suely Rolnik's description of Clark's art it seems clear that it was "perception" and "*the creative imagination*" as well as "the re-activation of this quality of *aesthetic experience* in the *receivers* of her creations"[162] that

101

were of central importance to Clark (my italics except for aesthetic experiences). In Clark we have perhaps for the first time an artist who for a while made issues such as choice and spectator participation and the creative moment central in her art, even though she soon drifted more and more into the realm of pedagogy.

Richardo Basbaum has described Clark's art as being about transformations and especially about moving the spectator from an essentially passive position to "the active and singular role of being the subject of your own experience."[163] Incidentally, this could also be a shorthand description of most psychodynamic psychotherapies. According to Guy Brett, "Clark believed that her work anticipated or accompanied a change in consciousness: that the whole cultural tradition in which we have projected our poetics outward onto a god figure or an artist figure was coming to an end, and that we would 'rediscover our own poetics in ourselves'."[164]

An important aspect of Clark's art was the connection to Mondrian (one is reminded here of Katarzyna Kobro in the 1920s and 1930s). According to Hélio Oiticica, who together with Clark and others was a driving force behind the Neo-constructivist Manifesto of 1959, "Lygia Clark did not limit herself to understanding superficially the 'geometrism' of Mondrian, but went back to the root of Mondrian's thought, generating insight into his most important lines of action, and opening a new way for art. Her primary comprehension is related to 'space', as the fundamental element tackled by Mondrian – not 'geometric form', as in the case of so many others. She understood the meaning of Mondrian's great intuitions, not from outside but from inside, as a living thing. Her need to 'verticalize' space, to 'brake the frame', for example, are not thought-out needs, or 'interesting' as an experiment, but highly aesthetic and ethical needs, surprisingly noble, placing her in relation to Mondrian like Cubism in relation to Cézanne."

Charlotte Posenenske

An artist that clearly must be considered of major importance to the development of Participatory Art was the German artist Charlotte Posenenske (1930-1985). In her art Posenenske went for an ever more radical simplification leading up to something that was very much akin to Minimal Art and recognized even at the time in the USA. But then she went further. In her last four works from 1967 and 1968 (she ceased making art in 1968 in order to pursue a career in sociology) the spectator was incorporated from the outset into the idea of the work and its execution.

In a statement published in Art International 1968 Posenenske wrote that "The things I make are/ variable/ as simple as possible/ reproducible.

They are components of space/ since they are like building elements, they can always be rearranged into new combinations or positions, thus, they alter space. I leave this alteration to the consumer who thereby again and anew participates in the creation".[165]

It is worth noticing that she uses the term "consumer" rather than "spectator" or any other term.

Interestingly enough, Posenenske's work resurfaced at the

Documenta 12 exhibition in 2007. In the catalogue she is mentioned as having "extended the spectrum of concrete Minimalist Art to include participatory and action components". The catalogue also informs us that in her works "Cooperative creativity replaces authoritarian artistic decision"; and also speaks of a "refusal of hierarchical composition" found "in changeability". On show at this 12th Documenta exhibition, apart from about ten other works mostly on paper, there were also three works with a clear participatory intent. One was a 2007 reconstruction of *Drehflügel (Revolving Vanes) Serie E* from 1967/68. One version of this might be described as a cube 100x100 cm with no top and with all sides opening like doors at the discretion of the spectator. Another version was 200 cm tall. These seems to be more of a classical transformable albeit on a larger scale.

The two other works, also large, *Vierkantrohre (Square Tubes) Serie D* and *Vierkantrohre Serie DW* from 1967, were more of a clear cut Participatory Art kind. In their appearance they reminded one of standard metal ventilation shaft segments. The artist had a clear intent that the segments should be combined and recombined using nuts and bolts by "the exhibitor, the buyer, or the public".

So typical for how scattered the field of Participatory Art has been and still is – it was not until 2007, when I first saw her entry in the catalogue of the 12th Documenta exhibition in Kassel - that I got to know of her Participatory Art activities (she never used that description, however).[166]

To sum up: the 1950s and 1960s were basically a revival

of tendencies that first emerged during and right after WW I. Perhaps that is not all that surprising as only around 20 years passed between the end of WW I and the beginning of WW II. We also need to remember that the major innovative art movements at this time – American expressionism, Pop Art, etcetera – did not have much relevance for Participatory Art. They were still very much about "retinal art". Those forms of art dominated the scene for decades. From the point of view of Participatory Art, the real strides forward during the 1950s and early 1960s were first of all the renewed emphasis on Mobile Art, mainly because this kept alive the idea of the open-ended work of art. Secondly, we saw the emergence of Multi Art, which kept alive the idea of the value of art without auteur, of art being something more than a signature of commercial interest. Thirdly, some artists explored a migration of art away from the art institutions and into the surrounding society – it seems, partly to avoid the dictates of and identification with the art market and partly out of a search for new aspects or deeper strata of reality.

PART IV

NOT JUST IN SCULPTURE

Participatory Art and paintings/pictures

Participatory Art has, so far in this discussion, been almost synonymous with a new kind of sculpture. But what about Participatory Art and the broader concept of art? Is participation possible to combine with other visual arts like painting and photography? Paul Klee claimed in 1924 that "The artist.....puts greater emphasis on the creative powers than on the forms these result in."

At first one may think that participation in painting is surely not possible. Maybe that is also true in some ways, but not altogether. In his fascinating and extremely scholarly book *Potential Images. Ambiguity and Indeterminacy in Modern Art*,[167] professor Dario Gamboni shows that for centuries painters tried different ways of increasing the involvement of the spectator. They did so not in the physical making of the painting, that is true, but in the "reading" of the painting. The spectator's *imaginative participation* was desired. Deliberate ambiguity and a general indeterminacy on the part of the painters were the major means to reach this end. There was "*a transfer of agency* from the artist to the spectator" as Gamboni points out.[168] (My italics). The danger seems to me, however, that this kind of art would become more of an intellectual challenge than an original visual communication. This kind of art seems to have reached its peak in France during the latter half of the 19ᵗʰ century with prominent artists like Paul Gauguin and Odilon Redon in the forefront and then leading through Cubism (with its emphasis on seeing) to both abstract art and to Marcel Duchamp.[169] "What Redon produces belongs both to the perceived object and to the perceiving mind and maintains itself on the fringes of both" according to Gamboni, who also quotes Redon describing his drawings and paintings of bouquets as "flowers from the meeting-point of two shores, representation and memory." Gamboni continues to say: "His [Redon's] favorite terms for his art and the effect he wants to produce on the spectator are suggestion, ambiguity and indeterminacy" while Redon is quoted as saying: "My drawings *inspire* and cannot be defined. They determine nothing. They place us, as music does, in the ambiguous world of indeterminacy."[170]

From the point of view of Participatory Art, the limitations of this kind of spectator participation are revealed, I believe, by Gamboni's words above: "the effect he wants to produce *on* the spectator". On commenting on the works of a couple of other important painters of the same period, Vuillard and Sérusier, Gamboni states that their works "are rather like puzzles."[171] Perhaps this best sums up the dangers, from a Participatory Art point of view with the whole "imaginative participation" type of painting: it constantly runs the risk of becoming an intellectual guessing game.

For centuries, spectators have to some extent been involved in the painting "coming into being" by the way the artist built up the painting along certain lines that steered the spectator's way of reading a painting, for example by drawing "hidden images" or by the calculated use of diagonals. This latter way of involving the spectator has been used in modern times by Josef Albers: "Looking at my *Structural Constellations* demands repeated transformations (changes) of viewing and reading directions. We follow the lines and then look from top to bottom and from left to right, read along the stretch of the figures, but also penetrate through them, forwards and backwards, here and there."... "The intention is that the object does not move, it moves us."[172]

The key to understanding spectator participation in pictures, however, is to acknowledge "the extraordinary *ability the viewer has of 'completing' a painting,* of reading space, volume and detail into flat forms."[173] to use an expression from Paul Greenhalgh (my italics); and, I would add, read subjective meaning into pictures. This is true to a greater or lesser extent of the scenes on Greek vases, Fayoum portraits, Medieval murals, Renaissance perspective landscapes and to an even greater extent of the reduced figuration of some of the symbolist painters, Matisse's single line drawings and much of Modernist painting. Like Dario Gamboni, Paul Greenhalgh has pointed out Vuillard as an early example of an artist demanding completion from the spectator. "His art, alongside the whole range of Impressionist and Post-Impressionist practice, was *relational,* in that its simplicity gained full meaning only when interpreted in terms of things the artist does not provide us with. Vuillard's bed, Gauguin's fields and Degas' jackets only work when we compare them to beds, fields and jackets we know. Indeed, the paintings demand that of us."[174]

Cézanne, towards the end of the 19th century, changed the relationship between painting and spectator by not dishing up a perfect image of what the artist saw, but rather inviting the spectator to share in *the problematic process of seeing* in itself. Cézanne emphasized the almost arbitrary relativity in deciding, consciously or subconsciously, what we see. The crucial word in understanding seeing in this way – which incidentally is also the way science has understood seeing since about that time – is the word "*deciding*". The word deciding implies *choice*. To my mind, this is simply another way of stating that seeing is also a *creative process*. Cézanne, with his ground breaking work, in particular from about 1890 until his death in 1906, realized *seeing as a creative process*. Impressionists like Manet and Monet were primarily interested in *making the spectator see reality as they thought it was at the very moment then and there,* as opposed to ideals and conventions about reality. In doing so they enlarged the scope of art in general and of painting in particular. An opening up of painting took place which led to several radically new ways of painting – for example Fauvism, Cubism, Futurism, and Abstract Art – which all involved not only retinal effects, but also *the role of the spectator*.

Around the beginning of the 20th century, Matisse broke new ground by not painting what he – and others – could see of reality, but rather trying to paint his own emotional response to what he saw and communicating this by de-emphasizing the figurative aspect (unlike for example Goya). Today we are able to recognize the enormity of this parting from conventions and the implications it has had for our visual relationship to reality. Given the enormity of this effort maybe it is not surprising that Matisse did not take it one step further into abstract art, even though he came close to it a few times. Judging from a letter written in 1911, the artist's core endeavor lay in working toward creating the means of individual expression of her- or himself.[175] Yet, implicitly, this core experience was to be reserved for the artist and not shared as an experience with the spectator. Matisse was unquestionably among those who, at the beginning of the 20th century, revolutionized painting and our way of looking at the world around us. He was, however, not trying to revolutionize the role of the artist as the active explorer, nor change the relationship between the artist, being active, and the spectator, being essentially passive. Eventually, however, some artists also tried to change these conditions in painting.

In his now classical panorama of the Modern Movement in art, Robert Hughes wrote: "The spectator, Boccioni declared in one of the Futurist *manifesti* (1912) 'must in the future be placed in the centre of the picture', exposed to the whole surrounding jabber of lines, planes, light, and noise that Futurism extracted from its motifs. This meant doing away with the painting as a proscenium, 'the small square of life artificially compressed'."[176] To this I would add that Boccioni also put the spectator in a quite different role. This *new role for of the spectator* was something of a hallmark of Modernism. The spectator needed to complete the picture, now that naturalism, representation, and central perspective were gone, replaced with mere flat surfaces and various experiments with colors. This meant spectators had to shift from the act of grasping and meditating to the process of seeing and making something out of what they saw. The spectator now more than ever before had to use his or her own creativity to come to grips with the painting. Cézanne was perhaps the first to give the spectator this new role with his nude "flat" female figures, followed by Matisse and even further emphasized by Cubism. Cubism, as have been mentioned earlier, had an enormously transformative effect on painting, not least in demanding a higher degree of participation of the spectator in completing the picture. A prime example, and indeed the first one, is Picasso's *Les Demoiselles d'Avignon* from 1907, now displayed at the Modern Museum of Art in New York.[177]

In 1916 Jean (Hans) Arp started his now famous series of collages where bits of colored paper were arranged on a background paper "according to the laws of *chance*" (my italics) although in a type of grid form. By mixing *accidentalness* (dropping pre-made, squar-ish pieces of paper onto a surface and then probably rearranging them somewhat in a ready-made structure – the grid pattern), Arp would "displace agency from artistic production" and to some extent also authorship. "What results is a work of art that is non-intentional, or at least complexly intentional, *where the artist exiles himself from the work he produces.*"[178] (My italics). To some extent, the same artistic strategy is also at play in Participatory Art, where the pieces designed and/or made or found by the artist are rearranged by the "spectator" into a pattern of his/her choice but not necessarily a pre-set pattern like a grid. Arp's method seems akin to T S Eliot's "fixity and flux" in poetry from roughly the same time[179].

Around 1919, Max Ernst began making pictures using pre-made imprints from the printing industry mixed with his own additions in drawing and painting. "The result was a visual puzzle that *requires the viewer to create* an ambiguous narrative around interconnected pictorial and linguistic signs..."[180] (My italics). With its connection here to the narrative, the spectator was invited to some kind of participation, a little bit further than the completion of the picture in early Modernism, or the more traditional contemplation of the picture.

Piet Mondrian played a key role in developing the participatory aspects of painting. Already in his first Paris studio, the one he built up in 1919 on rue de Coulmiers, Mondrian put colored sheets of cardboard directly onto the wall where he could then move them around. This was a technique, sometimes called "wall works", that he repeated in his now famous studio in rue de Départ between 1921 and 1936 and again in his New York studio from 1943 until his death in 1944. On the whole, Mondrian's opening up of the painting beyond the canvas (see for example his composition with four yellow lines, 1933) signified not only a new position, but perhaps also a somewhat new role for the spectator. The Swedish painter Ragnar Sandberg wrote in his diary in March 1945: "You should not cover up anything, because then you will prevent the spectator from following the coming into being of the work of art."[181] The process of a work of art coming into being hence had a value in itself and perhaps a value on par with the end product! In August 1948, Sandberg prophesized that "One day we will become bored with the tin soldiers that are cast for us, we will wish to see for ourselves the boiling tin moving around in the cauldron and imagine what can become of it. *We will no longer believe in the finished cast, in the completed process.*"[182] (My italics). And in 1959: "In the spectator there is always a development of energy going on. To some extent *it is in the hand of the creator to free this energy in any direction he would like to.* An artist, who makes pictures that give a disorganized and improvised impression, will create, in the spectator, a need for order and logical effect on his senses." And further: "In any case *the spectator is always a participant that falls into affect.*" [183] And: "It is not the author who should create the images, he should with his tools *get the reader to create those images* out of his written text."[184] (My italics and my translations).

Matisse was convinced that, from time to time in art history, it is necessary to "turn back from complexity and refinement to the beginnings of human perception in pure color, shape and movement – 'materials that stir the senses' – elementary principles that give life by coming alive themselves."[185], according to his insightful biographer Hilary Spurling. Matisse used this very technique in 1931 when building up his mural *The Dance* for the Barnes Collection in Philadelphia. This technique might perhaps be regarded as a kind of proto-Participatory Art for use only by Matisse himself: A hired house painter was charged with painting big sheets of paper in colors that Matisse had chosen. Matisse then cut out the shapes and had an assistant "pinning, shifting and re-pinning [onto the wall] *a composition that was perpetually on the move*"[186] (My italics), according to instructions delivered via a long bamboo stick, used by Matisse standing on the floor. "A composition made up of parts that were perpetually on the move" makes the process akin to Participatory Art, whereas, of course, the fact that Matisse alone made every choice and then froze the final results prevented it from being Participatory Art. But then participation was not his intention. He later used the same technique for his painting *The Pink Nude*, (1935), The Nelson Rockefeller decorative panel *Le Chant* (1938), illustrations to the magazine *Verve* (1940)[187], *The Fall of Icarus* (1943), that remarkable book *Jazz* (1943-44),[188] his studio wall in Vence covered in cut-outs, around 1945, *Oceania* and *Polynesia* (1946), the interiors of La Chapelle de Vence, as well as all his subsequent cut-out works, until his death in 1954.[189] Matisse also used a similar technique in creating The Emperor's Cloak for the ballet Le Chant du Rossignol (1919).

Matisse's interest in caged birds in strong colors began in Paris in 1936.[190] Eventually his birds grew in numbers so that within a few years he possessed about 300 birds, kept in a room of their own, with a keeper attending to them on a daily basis.[191] I wonder if he saw his birds as colors perpetually on the move, similar to his technique of moving round pieces of cut-out paper, or with the sun shining through the colored window panes in the chapel in Vence and moving the colors projected onto the largely black and white interior as the sun's rays progressed during the day.

Between 1938-1948, Matisse used sets of six dresses in various shapes and colors on his models as a basic working kit. "Matisse used them in much the same way as he used sheets of colored paper pinned to his canvases. Both supplied him with *building blocks capable of being combined and recombined* in the designs constructed from patches of flat color that still preoccupied him…"[192] (My italics). This sounds as an exact description of what a Participatory Art painter might be doing!

In the 1950s Vasarely took this method of building blocks one step further (but not necessarily in a more interesting direction) through reduction and geometrical forms creating a kind of visual alphabet called "plastic unit." By varying the colors and shapes of these units (for example small circles within squares) as well as the backgrounds, he could achieve an endless variety. Oddly enough, though the scene thus was set for creating Participatory Art with these tools, the possibility of doing so seems never to have been of main interest to Vasarely.

Spectator involvement in the creation of the work of art was more a matter of the brains' reaction to the optical phenomena, than in the compositions themselves; as, for example, seen in Vasarely's pictures. But as the image was in the brains of the beholders, there was *no image that could be called an original one*. Hence, it did not make sense to limit the starting point that Vasarely had established, by publishing numbered editions. This in turn was seen as a step in the direction of popularization of art.[193] This development happened to be very much in line with the spirit of post WW II neo-avantgardistic thinking. This thinking saw new possibilities in building an art upon the foundations of the emerging new technologies, rather than seeing the role of art as struggling against industrial production or adding value to industrial products, through design as had Moholy-Nagy's from the mid 1930s onwards.[194] (These designs perhaps culminated in his now classical Parker Pen in 1944-46.) Maybe it is not by coincidence that the black and white paintings exhibited by another Op-Art pioneer, Bridget Riley, at the *Responsive Eye* exhibition in New York, 1965, and at the Richard Feigen Gallery, were immediately turned into fabric patterns, even without the consent or knowledge of the artist[195].

Some artists, like Vasarely, Riley, Poons, Herbin, Baertling and Anuskiewicz were exploring perceptual phenomena like stroboscopic motion and afterimage. Though these phenomena of course depend on the willingness of the spectator to expose themselves to certain stimuli, art founded on those phenomena does not engage the spectator's own creativity and hence should not be considered Participatory Art. However, as an effort to highlight the role of the spectator in the making of art these phenomena are not without interest.

Both Calder (for example with *The White Frame* 1934) and Agam (in the early 1950s) experimented with mechanically powered paintings where the parts moved. So, too, did Tinguely and Richard Mortensen (in 1944). Mortensen seems to have incorporated the special sounds of his machines moving. He also seemed more oriented towards endless variations and emphasizing the accidental in art. In this kind of art, presumably the spectator could initiate electrically powered movements of elements in the pictures, by pressing a button. This did not offer much scope for the creativity of the spectator, but was perhaps an important step in the direction of the open-ended painting? Back in the 1930s, Calder created paintings intended to be seen from any angle, that is, without a particular up or down, in them, *thus leaving that choice to the spectator*; as did Gabo in the years 1935-46[196] and as Moholy-Nagy had done with his photographs in the 1920s.[197] Morris Louis continued this tradition in the 1952. According to several sources quoted by Gamboni "...the artist held this option open as long as possible while taking into account the opinions of critics, dealers, art lovers and collectors – after Louis's death in 1962, Greenberg was put in charge of this and deciding about the cutting up of canvases."[198]

In terms of physical participation of the spectator in a painting, Hans Richter tried out another variety on that theme in the 1950s. Richter, who together with Viking Eggling were among the pioneers of abstract film, appears to have worked with what Denise René called "peintures-rouleaux" – painting roles – "a bit like kakemonos" (my translation).[199] The idea resembles the story teller's scrolls of Rajasthan in India, except that in the case of Richter, the spectator operated the scroll on their own.

The real breakthrough of participatory painting (though of course that term did not exist at the time) came in the early 1960s with Öyvind Fahlström. Fahlström was of Swedish-Norwegian origin. He was raised in Brazil until the age of 10 when he was sent to Sweden to visit relatives and became separated from his parents by WW II. In 1961, he moved to New York. Fahlström was active as a concrete writer-poet-painter-journalist-translator with strong interests in music as well as in radical politics. In 1954 he wrote a manifesto for concrete poetry (*Hätila ragulpr på fåtskliaben*) It is worth mentioning Fahlström's varied background and disparate interests because it may explain why he seems to have been the first artist to combine figurative painting and some thinking akin to Participatory Art. He did this in a number of what he called variable paintings, starting with *Sitting...Six months later, version A* from 1962, *The Planetarium* (1963), *Babies for Africa* (1963) and *The Cold War* (1963-1965).[200] The idea was that the spectators were invited to manipulate some elements of the variable paintings. To someone who was affected during his youth by traumatic events beyond his control, the idea of game theory, of rules to be transgressed and ability to manipulate the world at will must have held a strong attraction. The freedom to play here was as important as the creative act of the artist, as Suely Rolnik pointed out.[201] In some of his variable paintings Fahlström used the concept of "game" as in *Sitting Dominoes* from 1966 (reproduced on the cover of Art News the same year), *World Trade Monopoly (B, large)* and *Pentagon Puzzle* both from 1970 and *Kidnapping Kissinger* (1972). During the last couple of years of his life he reverted to the abstraction of his early variables with works like *At Five in the Afternoon* (1974) and the almost entirely abstract and partially variable painting from the year before his death *Night Music 2: Cancer Epidemic Scenario* (1975). "The artist even sought to express a 'temporal form of image' in his paintings, not possible to grasp as an entirety in one glance, but as results of situations and events. The variable paintings of the 1960s and onwards can thus be seen as an attempt to bring art closer to music and theater", according to Teddy Hultberg[202].

His variable paintings apart, Fahlström also produced a few works of art that Mike Kelley has referred to as "horizontal paintings." Sometimes they also appear to be called "installations", for example, Fahlström's first two "pool" paintings *Parkland Memorial* and *The Little General,* both from 1967 and the *Dante –Virgil Skating Race* (1968 and shown at the *Documenta IV* in Kassel, Germany[203]). These were made up of various figures or signs he had painted on items floating around in pools of water. Here, the source of movement was either the spectator or the draft in the room, leaving less room for the creativity of the spectator and more room for chance.

Fahlström also made a few installations like the non-variable *Dr Schweitzer's Last Mission* (1962 and exhibited at the Venice Biennale in 1966), the variables *World Bank* (1972) and *At Five in the Afternoon* (1974) amongst others.

Another way of looking at Öyvind Fahlström's art is to say that he explored, or was preoccupied with, how bits and pieces of various kinds, but with certain elements of identity in common, could be handled in a fruitful manner, either by the artist and/or the spectator – a kind of mobile collages. One is reminded of the delight in a child who discovers meaning in putting syllables and words together when learning to read. Indeed, the left panel of Fahlström's diptych *The Planetarium* from 1963 is made up of words much like the magnetic words people now play with on their fridges. Fahlström also described with approval how the descriptions in Nathalie Sarraute's novel with the same name[204] had "been ground down into tiny fragments floating round each other in the same confusing apparent disorder like heavenly bodies in a planetarium."[205] Yet, exactly because these fragments were just floating around haphazardly, they were "producing an unusually close experience of a human being". The repeated, yet disparate, varied and interrelated patterns and colors of comic strips also seem to have fascinated him. Perhaps again there was a semblance to his own life experience. In any case, the step to making variable paintings was perhaps not all that big a step for Fahlström.

In a brief text called *A Game of Character* from 1964, Fahlström tried to explain the new turn his painting had taken towards being *variable paintings*.[206] "The basic element in my picture is the 'character-form' by which I mean an 'abstract' form of a particular individual shape, conspicuous as character, as a type form, regardless of varying proportions, color shades, other style qualities etc." ... "The association of disparate elements to each other thus makes game rules and the work of art will be a game structure. This among other things, leads to presupposing *an active, participating spectator* (my italics) who – whether he is confronted with a static or a variable work of art – will find relations which will make him able to 'play' the work, while the elements that he does not relate and in general his individual decomposition make for chance, the uncertainty that, when clashing with the 'rules' create the thrill of a game."

The idea of *basic recurring elements* had been used by Fahlström in earlier paintings. In his first variables, however, in paintings like *Sitting...Blocks* (1965-1966) and *Sitting...Dominoes* (1966) mainly certain lines, patterns and colors recur on identical shapes that the spectator can then connect in any way he or she desires.

In *Sitting...(1962),* Fahlström's first variable painting, the spectator is permitted to "introduce circulation into the juxtapositions of niches or 'panels' – to use the term of the comic books – that define the pictorial grid."[207] In 1967, he created the mobiles *Parkland Memorial* and *The Little General" (Pinball Machine)* where the water surface becomes the canvas (hence pool paintings) and where artifacts by Fahlström drifted around, steered only by *chance* or – I suppose, though this was never emphasized by Fahlström – by intervention from the spectator. The quality sought was more like what happens in dreams.

Fahlström's great contribution to Participatory Art in painting was to prove – albeit inadvertently – that Participatory Art does not necessarily have to be constructivist in kind, but could even be figurative! I describe it as happening inadvertently, because, for Fahlström, despite being both a highly theoretically interested and theoretically motivated person, the participatory aspect of his variable paintings seem to be based less on an interest in *the participatory creative experience of the spectator,* or in the particular value of getting the spectator to leave his or her passive role, as much as it was based on a new dimension in his own comments on the world, its accidental quality. Indeed, as Mike Kelley observed, "The variable artworks were generally shown alongside related 'fixed' pieces that revealed its various 'phases' – preferred arrangements of the variable paintings *determined by the artist* (my italics) – as well as sketches that shed light on their source materials."[208]

Neither Agam nor Fahlström dedicated their art exclusively to variable sculpture or variable paintings or any other form akin to Participatory Art. In 1963 Fahlström wrote: "I'm mainly interested in *'making paintings that are worlds by manipulating the world'* by creating and relating *models* of the world; not *symbols* – anyone may put in whatever he finds – only he sees (some of) the relations: what is like, unlike, repeated, juxtaposed, etc., etc."[209] Fahlström seemed more interested in game theory as an expression of the bipolar world of the 1960s as well as "the protest folklore of the 60s and its procedures of diverting advertising language." [210]

One can only surmise why artists like Agam et al did not pursue interactive painting, or Participatory Art in general, despite having made quite a few spectacular works of art in that vein. The answer, I believe, is to be found in a lack of theoretical interest in the foundations for what they were then doing, as well as in the restrictions inherent in the nature of Participatory Art, in view of what they wished to achieve. Fahlström did make a number of variable paintings, but for reasons other than an interest in exploring the creativity of the spectator or creativity as such.

Participatory Art and photography

In a comment on an article on painting and photography, Mondrian, with his firm rooting in Neo-Plasticism, wrote that to him photography seemed "rather more imitative than plastic in character." To him photography was "the appropriate means for *reproduction* of objectivity" whereas "all art is *creation.*" What prevented Mondrian from seeing the potentials of a new kind of photography I think was his traditional conception of the role of the artist: ... "one must not overlook the fact that the 'artist,' not the 'means,' [that] creates the work of art." In other words, thoughts of the role of the spectator did not enter the mind of Mondrian. Despite his expressed radical ambitions to break down conventions in art – he called his Neo-Plasticism "destructive-constructive",[211] in his views on the role of the artist he was still trapped in a convention. To his credit, though, he kept an open mind: "...it is difficult at present [i.e.1927] to predetermine the evolution of photography – indeed such great accomplishments have been realized in the realm of pure plastic that everything may also be expected of photography. It is quite possible that the technique of photography will change, just as the technique of painting has changed."[212]

The reader will be excused if he or she has the impression that surely such a "fixed medium" as still photography can not be used in any way that resembles Participatory Art. Or, can it? It can be said that the early roots of Participatory Art in photography is to be found in the later much despised tendency called pictorialism, with its relationship to Impressionism. There are other early forerunners, as well.

In theory one could make Participatory Photographs by providing kits for making cameraless photograms - putting objects onto photographically sensitive film and exposing the work to daylight, similar to Christian Schad's Shadographs (1918-1919) and Man Ray's Rayographs (somewhat later).[213] This, however, would be to skirt the issue a bit, because from a photographic point of view, the restrictions would be extremely limiting. The famous

Swedish author's "*celestographs*" and "*chrystallizations*" from the 1890s might be considered an even earlier case in point. At that time Strindberg even wrote an essay called "Chance in Artistic Creation".

Or, one could emulate the cut-and-paste tradition, popular in Germany during WW I and a forerunner to the photomontages so typical of the Berlin Dadaists around 1920[214] and the photo sculptures (as he called them, himself) by Moholy-Nagy in the 1920s.[215] But in this case, would not the end product be exactly photomontages rather than photographs? They would, unless, of course, one combined them with the technique developed by the painter Öyvind Fahlström and made moveable photomontages.

If we talk about photography in the traditional sense, intuitively we may assume that photography – given its "fixity" is far away from Participatory Art, except for the fact that just like in painting, the photographic work of art to some extent is also created in the mind of the spectator. This begs the question: What would make a certain photograph more rather than less a work of Participatory Art? This question is difficult to answer.

But if we are to follow the model in painting put forward by Dario Gamboni of "ambiguity and indeterminacy", then it seems to me that for photographs to be participatory photographs to a large extent would depend on the spectator completing the picture. "Indeterminacy" would provide more scope for participatory photographs than "ambiguity". Participatory photography would have to focus on *the zone between the abstract and the realistic* – or more specifically *on the oscillation between them*. To my mind at least, this is a highly interesting zone in it self to explore. The participation possibilities in these kinds of pictures might, however, be more akin to the participation offered by music. The symbolist painter Odilon Redon, compared his paintings to music rather than paintings depicting something specific.

Are we perhaps caught in the chronology of concepts when we describe this zone between the abstract and the realistic as an in-between zone? Perhaps it rather represents a closer mirroring of reality than either of the two. It might be so. And maybe both the purely realistic rendering and the purely abstract rendering represent more "primitive" states of perception? I say, primitive in the sense of coming to us earlier in our development as human beings.

From the point of view of Participatory Art, photos taken from the zone in between realistic rendering and abstract pattern leave the spectator the option to see them one way or the other, or both, switching at will. This gives the spectator one of the most fundamental tools for creating and for making art and Participatory Art in particular, namely, *choices to be made*. It is also possible to take this one step further and take photographs that seem to be neither representative nor entirely abstract. Furthermore, this creative role of the spectator relates to the Conceptual Art of the 1960s claiming that a work of art lay not in its execution but in its concept as an idea that either could be executed or left with the "spectator." Although, this kind of in-between photography may make it easier for the viewer to shape something out of her/his imaginations into something of aesthetic value – or meaning – to her/

him.

As a painter, Matisse came close to abstract painting, yet never really crossed the line. The net result seems to have been more of a fusion of the two tendencies. A fusion, however, is not the same as creating *a zone in-between* the two perspectives. In such a zone, the tension of both perspectives is still alive and the resolution of this tension takes place *within the spectator* to the extent that the spectator is willing to stay with that challenge. In the fusion of the two perspectives, the challenge is resolved by the artist. An amalgamation results, that may be interesting or pleasing, but does not leave the same creative challenges and *choices* to the spectator. With Synthesism (a synthesis of impression, line and color), as he then called it, Gauguin had also tried to explore the zone between abstraction and realism in paintings like *Seascape with cow* (1888), by stressing emotive line and color. His concern, however, was how to reproduce nature rather than the choice offered to the spectator. As mentioned above, Vuillard was another artist working on the border between the abstract and the representative.

And then there is, of course, Moholy-Nagy, again.[216] His photographs "stood out by their unusual framing and camera angles (close-ups, bird's eye and worm's eye views, and diagonal compositions). They became models of the so-called Neues Sehen (New vision) in the photography of the 1920s. They are not realistic in the sense of striving for an objective portrayal of reality, but rather are an example of 'using and testing Constructivist theories of perception and composition....' ". [217] From a participatory point of view, Moholy-Nagy's photographs challenge the spectator to see in them either a motif or a pattern or switching between the two *at will and thus again to have a choice*. The same technique is evident in the photography of several of the other people who were at the Bauhaus,[218] not least in the photos of Joseph Albers, a teacher colleague at the Bauhaus, even though Albers seems to have taken his photographs more for personal usage than for publication[219].

From the point of view of Participatory Art, Albers' photographs are of particular interest. "Albers recognized visual perception as not just a physiological but also a psychological process, the interaction between the two determining how the mind 'interprets' the retinal image." And "… in Albers' photographs the moment of truth resides not so much in any one shot as in the negative 'unseen' space in-between. Demanding *the active participation of the viewer* to fill this space…"[220] (my italics).

A special feature with some of Moholy-Nagy's photographs was that there was no obvious up or down built into some of the pictures. A picture like *In the Sand* could be turned around by the spectator holding the picture in her or his hands and thus *choosing* a personally preferred angle.[221]

What has made photography so difficult to combine with Participatory Art is of course its static nature. With the advent of the electronic medium, however, I believe this can – and indeed also will – change. One day, someone will start making "open photos" that someone else continues with. The real limitation will probably still be the relatively limited physical involvement demanded of the "spectator".

Are Installations, Happenings and Environmental Art also Participatory Art?

Wagner had his ideas of the *Gesamtkunstwerk* appealing to the visual and to the auditive as well as to the verbal drama. Was this also serving as a source of inspiration to the earliest examples of Installations? Perhaps the first installation might be said to be Marcel Duchamp's studio in New York about 1916-21[222] or to Kurt Schwitters' *Merzbau* (1919-1937) – his home turned into a sculpture of sorts – or to the Cologne Dada Fair which you entered through a public toilet (April 1920).[223] The Exposition Internationale du Surréalism (Paris 1938) was another early exhibition turned into an installation. Piet Mondrian's studio in 1926 on rue du Départ that he showed to people as a "Neo-Plastic work" was another studio shown as a work of art. Then, perhaps it was Ed Lissitzky's *Proun Room* made in 1923, for the *Grosse Berliner Kunstausstellung* that was the first installation only. *Proun Room* was a combination of room and constructivist paintings that taken together formed a work of art which spectators entered into. The main interesting feature was what was inside, however.[224] Schwitters himself, however - at least in 1936 - saw his *Merzbau* as a sculpture: "I am building an abstract (cubist) sculpture into which people can go."[225] Though, in reality, it seems to have been as much a monumental assemblage. By 1936, his sculpture had also broken out through the house he lived in. Walter Benjamin also seems to have regarded it as "a sculpture into which people can go."[226] Not having seen it in reality (it no longer exists) I find it difficult to tell if it really had an exterior. If so, did this by definition make it into an installation rather than a sculpture? Perhaps the work of art began as an installation but evolved into something that could be regarded both as an installation and a sculpture – the difference being the different requirements made on the public? Unfortunately – and ironically – *Merzbau* was destroyed during WW II. Ironically, because WW I, more than anything, set Schwitters on his artistic path.

One could argue that Happenings as such were pioneered by the Futurist Filippo Marinetti[227] (for example, *Variety Theater,* 1913). Much of the "technique" was later incorporated by the Dadaists like the Zurich Dadaists (Hugo Ball at the *Cabaret Voltaire* in 1916 for example), the *Manifestation Dada* 1920 and Tristan Tzara's *Soirée du Coer à Barbe* in 1923, and perhaps even the Dadaist/ surrealist mock trial of Maurice Barrés by André Breton and others in Paris on May 13, 1921. Denise René, the gallery owner so highly important for the development of modern art, mentioned in an interview that the artist Jean Hérold, before WW II, organized a kind of happenings tableaux-vivante-style in his studio in Montparnasse.[228]

Maybe the spirit of experimenting, so close to the spirit of entrepreneurship, gave Happenings such an appeal to some Americans after WW II. In one of the Black Mountain "evenings" in 1952, John Cage together with Robert Rauschenberg, Franz Kline, the poet Charles Olson and choreographer Merce Cunningham staged *Theater Piece No. 1,* which probably was the first staged "happening" in America unless one counts in Duchamp's studio in New York 1916-21. The American artist Allan Kaprow began in 1956 with his series of *environments*

(*Penny Arcade*) and collage-like *installations* (*Rearrangeable Panels* from 1957-59) which later developed into *happenings* (*18 Happenings in 6 Parts* from 1959). The aim, however, seems to have gone in the direction of increasing involvement of the audience in some kind of performance intended to explore the nature of art, rather than in exploring any specific form of plastic art. Hence this kind of art is of less interest to Participatory Art, save the fact that it shows another early trend in society toward increased "spectator" participation.[229]

Reflecting the internationalization of the art world, the Fluxus movement (by some said to have flourished between 1962-1978, but by others claimed to still exist) consisted of many artists from both the United States and Europe (including John Cage, Allan Kaprow and Joseph Beuys). Fluxus was a very loosely connected radical movement intended to simultaneously free art from its ties to unique and highly valued objects and to set free the *creativity of ordinary people*. Hence its followers took an interest in both happenings and Multi Art. We will come back to Beuys further on.

In 1966, Niki de Saint Phalle in collaboration with Jean Tinguely and P-O Ultvedt constructed *She* (Hon – en katedral) at the Museum of Modern Art in Stockholm, Sweden. The public was invited to physically enter a giant sculpture of a reclining woman created on site, for that purpose (as opposed to more vaguely delimited installations). The intention was that people would experience this sculpture fully, by entering inside the sculpture, as was also the later art work by Robert Stackhouse : *Running Animals, Reindeer Way (1976).* By contrast, people can also enter the Statue of Liberty in New York, but neither the inside nor the fact that people enter it has any particular artistic meaning. Entering into a work of art is definitely a different experience from looking at art on the wall or taking in a sculpture by looking at it and walking around it.

Participation in the early 1960s - Hélio Oiticica and David Medalla

Any book on Participatory Art would have to include at least a mentioning of Hélio Oiticica (1937-1980) and David Medalla (1942-); if only because they seem to have been among the first in the early 1960s to have deliberately sought to turn the spectator into a participant also in a physical sense. Their art was not, however, Participatory Art as conceived in this book with its focus on the creative moment, but rather the kind of participation inherent in environmental installations and happenings so typical of the 1960s. As was the case of several other artists at that time the participatory aspect was more in offering the spectators/participants physical and tactile involvement and the opportunity to sample a smorgasbord of mental and *sensory experiences* of a simpler or more complex kind to be sampled at will and stirring unspecified thoughts as well as emotions and ethical-social-political awareness.[230]

Hélio Oiticica was one of the followers of Lygia Clark and like her from Brazil and the Brazilian Neo-Concretist movement though his international reputation seems to stem largely from his major solo exhibition called the Whitechapel Experiment at the Whitechapel Art Gallery in London from 25 February to 6 April 1969. Mark

Glazebrook, at the time director of the gallery, refers to Oiticica's "environments" describing how "People poured in to take off their shoes, to 'tread the earth' and experience all sorts of new physical and mental sensations – new in an art gallery, at least." Others have described Oiticica's work as installations, performance and even Conceptual Art. In his choice of materials Oiticica seems to have much in common with his contemporary Pistolletto and others in the Arte Povera movement.

His most famous work is the installation *Tropicália PN2* and *PN3 1966-7* – "a landmark work of early installation art and a pivotal work for Oiticica himself" according to Tate Director Nicholas Serota. In explaining the background of *Tropicália* and its relation to his experience of the favelas of Rio, Oiticica summed up his intentions this way: "So two important elements in my own evolution counted for a great deal here. The first was the creation of an environment for behavior that would involve the 'works' and evolve in accordance with them. The second would refer to the participator's behaviour on direct contact with such an environment, and on the global perceptions of that behaviour. I don't want to isolate sensory or lived experience and so forth here; that would be the aesthetic side of the thing. What I want is to offer a global meaning that suggests a new behaviour, an ethical-social one that gives individuals a new sense of things". He also said that "In the larger Penetrable, the participator comes into contact with a multiplicity of experiences that refer to the image: tactility, furnished by elements available for manipulation; playfulness and the purely visual (patterns); and trajectory ('treading' would also be included in the tactility), until one arrives at the end of the labyrinth, in the dark, where a television is permanently switched on: the image absorbs the participator in the global accretion of information. I consider this to be an experimental exercise of the image, the experiential awareness attained by every individual who penetrates in that the world is a global thing".

Other works are large-scale installation *Eden* with a section called "myth opened area". Art critic and curator Guy Brett wrote about *Eden* that it "is not a manifestation of the artist's personal choices. There is nothing there to be deciphered. The value of these works is not *proved* by reference to some external interpretation. Like games, or rituals, we bring them into existence by involving ourselves. They are effective only in so far as we truly take part."

Penetrables and *Parangolé* were about color being "worn, handled and paraded" according to Guy Brett who in practical terms together with David Medalla and Paul Keeler introduced Oiticica to the London art world through the gallery *Signals* in London. (Medalla met both Lygia Clark and Oiticica in Paris in 1963).

Bolides were boxes and glass containers with pigment to be manipulated by the spectator/participant. As we can see Oiticica was stressing participation in a sensory experience rather than challenging the other person's creativity.

The group of six *Nest Cells* was "One of the most freely participatory features of *Eden*. These were large rectangular boxes, divided one from another by translucent curtains, to which people could bring whatever materials they liked to make a nest for themselves, habitable and personal."

Oiticica, it seems, was more interested in what surrounds creativity, maybe even the social preconditions for creativity, rather than the actual creative process in itself.

David Medalla's art has been of many differing kinds over the years. According to Richard Dyer in Frieze 1995 Medalla is "an artist for whom the visual is visionary and any material, or mode of expression, is valid". Apparently he is "constantly shifting his strategies and media; just when one thinks one has him pinned down as a situationist, a surrealist, or a conceptualist in the mode of Oldenburg – endlessly conceiving fantastic, unrealizable schemes – he changes direction and launches into a new direction".

According to the British art organization Iniva (Institute of International Visual Arts) he has moved between many kinds of art. "It has ranged anywhere from sculpture and Kinetic art to painting, installation and performance with all the spaces and overlaps between these forms". [231] During the late 1960s and early 1970s "Medalla made a series of 'participation works' where the audience was encouraged to be involved in the production of playful and experiential pieces which challenged the notions of creative hierarchy."

A participatory work of special interest for involving many participators individually over time is his *A Stich in Time* which is about "travel, time and chance, but also about production" according to Iniva. This work offered the audience the opportunity to stitch a small object of significance onto a large cloth in a public space. These still exist. So there seems to have been an end state sought after albeit one not planned in detail. "It is in the actual act of stitching, when you thread your own needle and start stitching, that you have your own space, your psychological space, apart from the physical space, and I find that very moving" Medalla is quoted as saying.

Though obviously participatory to some extent again this does not seem to be Participatory Art in the meaning put forward in this book but more in the sense of spectator involvement in a broader experiential sense.

Richard Serra (born in 1940) was part of a group that, according to Serra, included Eva Hesse, Bob Smithson and Bruce Nauman. "We were the down-and-dirty kids who came along with ugly, dirty material you had to walk around and walk through. That opened up the field."[232] Richard Serra's wonderful work later on, in gigantic undulating steel plates, *Torqued Ellipse,* serve as an example. At his retrospective at MoMA in 2007, spectators could walk in-between these walls of steel. From no point could the entire sculpture be seen as an entity. "There is no Gestalt reading" said Serra in an interview in connection with the exhibition.[233] The interviewer summed up the experience of his retrospective thus: "These blocks and toruses, ellipses, coils and spirals lay claim to the space and *invite your involvement* (my italics). As you walk into them, *you are no longer a spectator: you become the work* (my italics)." The interviewer here refers to involvement that implies just physical movement, apart, of course, from emotional response. From the Participatory Art point of view, Serra in 2007, however splendid his sculptures are, is only continuing to develop the installation form of art.

No mean feat in itself, but a walk-in-sculpture is more akin to installations than to Participatory Art.

The next step – a step not taken by any of the above mentioned installation artists – may be the work of art being created around the spectator by what the *spectator does beyond just moving her/himself*, once he or she has entered the premises made up by the work of art. We then have a somewhat interactive installation. The differentiator from art in general is that the art surrounds the spectator, rather like surround sound, but it would differ from the ordinary installation in that it would require some action on behalf of the spectator, in order to come fully into being. Only then would it be approaching Participatory Art.

Participatory Art, art pedagogy and educational toys

Progressive art pedagogy at the beginning of the 20th century was pointing in the direction of Participatory Art, but never directly developing that particular idea. It is worth mentioning though, because indirectly, progressive art may have influenced the beginnings of Participatory Art.

Already in 1905, Eugéne Grasset tried to demonstrate that new forms would emerge from the possibility of infinite variation of known reserves of forms. "To innovate is to preserve by modifying"[234] - a principle that would later be widely accepted at the Bauhaus as well, according to Rainer Wick.[235] A practical example would be rectangles painted with a pattern without any up or down and painted in such a way that any side would fit with any other side. Hence, these rectangles could be combined and recombined into larger patterns in many ways.[236]

"To liberate the creative forces and thereby the artistic talents of the students" was the explicit goal of Johannes Itten's teaching at the Bauhaus.[237]

As one of the sources for Itten's pedagogy, Rainer Wick mentions the well-known American philosopher John Dewey (1859-1952) who formulated pedagogy around "learning by doing". Dewey's ideas were taken up by Georg Kerschensteiner (1854-1932) who strove for a pedagogy aimed at seeing to "that each child discovered its own soul and produced that which was hidden dormant within it".[238]

One of the key elements of Johannes Itten's well-known teaching was the analysis of old masters, according to Wick. This analysis, far from being a dry anatomical dissection, took place through the student using various drawing techniques. The purpose of the exercise was for the students "to discover the essence of the painting *through their own creative act*" (my italics), according to Wick.[239] Understanding art through copying works of art was part of the traditional art pedagogy. But understanding art through using your own creativity?

To quote Wick further: "This means that Itten confronts the myth of the genius of *creation ex nilhilio* with the idea that the creative process consists of altering in innovative ways existing circumstances provided by God", "inventing form by transforming form, the artistic work of the Bauhaus student Kurt Kranz (1910-1997) is based largely on this principle."[240]

Participatory Art would go one step further, as I understand it – not only inviting spectators to understand art by using their own creativity, but also understanding creativity itself, as well as something essential about themselves, and through that also something important about being human.

Interestingly, these pedagogical toys keep on resurfacing again and again, particularly in museum shops all over the world. Sometimes they fall into the category of educational toys and sometimes they seem to be labeled executive toys or "little gadgets". The principle is the same, but they actually address two ends of the spectrum of the market. They are mainly differentiated by the materials they are made of. Educational toys seem to be most often made of plastic while executive toys mostly seem to be made of metal and often using magnetism. Both categories have in common the idea that there is someone interested in "playing" around with them, i.e. someone feels their creativity is enough challenged by these "toys" to desire fiddling with them. And it seems there always are. These toys never become great hits like Rubic's Cube, but on the other hand new versions have kept popping up again and again during the past four or five decades. I find it interesting that consistently over the years, a small percentage of customers seem interested enough to buy. Here again is a parallel to art. Any gallery owner can tell you that only a small percentage of the public is interested in abstract art, just as only a small percentage is interested in sculpture of any kind. So, the interest in abstract sculpture should be rather small, but consistent. The same seems to be the case with Educational Toys, Executive Toys, or Writing Desk Gadgets. Seen from another point of view, however, it is remarkable that people have a steady interest in having their aesthetic creativity challenged in that way.

Toys, it might be said, have always been "participatory". But educational toys have been more explicitly so, and in a more abstract approach. The oldest one I have seen was called Parquet, made of flat pieces of untreated wood in geometrical shapes. It probably dates from around the turn of the last century. But Parquet seemed more of a puzzle than an aesthetic challenge. Example of modern versions of Parquet with a clear aesthetic intent are the three dimensional DotyBlocs by David Doty in 1968 and the Anni Albers Magnetic Tiles. If this is an unfair statement, I apologize to Richard Doty who might have intended his DotyBlocs to be Participatory Art Multiples, but the demarcation line is not always all that clear. (Perhaps it should be defined by the freedom left open to the spectator?). Doty seems to have described his creation as "A system of changeable design".

Toys with only a participatory angle, without any higher aesthetic ambitions, have been around for a long time. We just have to think of Meccano, the rubber bricks that came out in England after the war and, of course, Lego. Educational toys with clearly both an *aesthetic* ambition *and* a *participatory* foundation seem to have been more rare. The earliest example I have come across is one called "Dandanah. The Fairy Palace", a set of 51 cast glass building blocks in various shapes and colors designed in 1919-20 by Bruno Taut (1880-1938) and manufactured in 1927. "In a literal way the blocks correspond to Taut's plea to man to *participate* in building utopia" (my italics).[241]

So what differentiates Participatory Art from edu-cational toys? I would say it is the absence of utilitarian purpose or perhaps one should say entertainment purpose. It is sometimes said that art is distinguished from craft by the latter being applied to utilitarian objects, whereas art is made without any utility in mind. Even the possible decorative effect of art should not be the primary drive behind its existence.

Conceptual Art and Participatory Art

It is sometimes said that Conceptual Art began as a parallel to – but also became the continuation of – Minimalism. They both share a questioning of the work of art as such, and of art in general. It has also been said, that there are connections between Conceptual Art and the Fluxus movement and hence also to performance art.

The reason for bringing up Conceptual Art in this context, however, is a different one. It is because Conceptual Art, like Participatory Art, in a serious way set out to expand *the role of the spectator*. Seeing, contemplating, even moving around a work of art was no longer enough. Instead, with Conceptual Art emerging in the 1960s, the spectator was now asked, *as an integral part of the art work,* to read, to figure out, to contextualize, and to respond to statements of various kinds.

This new role of the spectator, ascribed to a new kind of art, invites us to take a closer look at this art. What are the major similarities and differences between Conceptual Art and Participatory Art? Let us start with the similarities:

From Sol LeWitt's well-known essay explaining Conceptual Art in Artforum of June 1967, we note that there is, firstly, one similarity in that, in neither kind of art is *the final object* of crucial importance. (The same also applies to much that came out of the Fluxus movement). Conceptual Art, like Participatory Art, stresses *the work of art coming into being,* as opposed to perceptual art or "retinal art", for example any art that is based on color, optical sensations, or movement. In Conceptual Art, *what the work of art finally looks like is not terribly important.* Hence the craftsmanship of the artist is not of great interest either. What is important, however – and here there is yet another great similarity with Participatory Art – is *the process of conception of the work of art.* LeWitt points out that perceptual art and conceptual art are inherently contradictory – one being "postfact", the other "prefact", as he so aptly put it. If the final object is not of central concern to Conceptual Art, the *process of conception* is all the more so. And, central to the conception, according to LeWitt, is the *idea* as well as *intuition.* "If the artist carries through his idea and makes it into visible form, then all the steps in the process are of importance. The idea itself, even if not made visual, is as much a work of art as any finished product. All intervening steps – scribbles, sketches, drawings, failed works, models, studies, thoughts, and conversations – are of interest. Those that show that the thought process of the artist are sometimes more interesting than the final product ". "Conceptual Art is good only when the idea is good."[242] And "ideas are discovered by intuition", LeWitt also claimed. Independently of any form a work of art might have, it will have started with an *idea.*

Both Conceptual Art and Participatory Art are apparently mainly focusing on the very *process of the work of art coming into being*, regarding it as important a part of the work as any other, rather than focusing on the final outcome or the craftsmanship of the artist. "What the work of art looks like isn't terribly important" said LeWitt. Participatory Art, on the other hand – and herein lies an important difference – is focused on the spectator's *subjective experience* of aesthetic *choices to be made* (and not yet made) within the creative process as such.

One could say that Participatory Art is the one kind of art that, more than any other kind of art, conveys to the spectator *the experience* of (not an illustration of) the fundamental existential human dilemma of *choice*, with all the implications this has for our identity, as described by the philosopher Kirkegaard already in the middle of the 19th century.

The role of choice is not unimportant to Conceptual Art, but it engages a different kind of choice, according to LeWitt: "If the artist wishes to explore his idea thoroughly, then the arbitrary or chance decisions would be kept to a minimum, while caprice, taste, and other whimsies would be eliminated from the making of art."[243] LeWitt seems to be talking more about the choices of the artist than the choice of the spectator, just as Duchamp did some 50 years earlier. For Participatory Art on the contrary, the important choices are those of the spectator/participant. Cutting-edge industry today calls this "user insights" and sees it as something extremely valuable.

A highly important similarity would be that in both forms

of art the artist *relinquishes control over the end result.* In LeWitt's words: "Once it is out of his hand the artist has no control over the way a viewer will perceive the work. Different people will understand the same thing in a different way". In Participatory Art different people will *use/finalize* the participatory work of art in different ways.

In his 1967 article in Artforum, LeWitt also states something that is highly pertinent to Participatory Art: "*When an artist uses a multiple modular method he usually chooses a simple and readily available form. The form itself is of very limited importance; it becomes the grammar for the total work.*" (My italics). And also:"Using a simple form repeatedly narrows the field of the work and concentrates the intensity to the arrangement of the form. This arrangement becomes the end while the form becomes the means". How typical this way of working is for Conceptual Art I can not tell, but it seems highly relevant for Participatory Art, at least in its sculptural form.

Finally both forms of art have one more trait in common: *The problem of ascribing to them a material value* and, as part of this problem, how they relate to the problem encountered by Multi Art; are they works of art in many originals, or is there one original work of art and the rest are all copies? For Conceptual Art, the problem deepens with LeWitt's comment that "The idea itself, even if not made visual, is as much a work of art as any finished product." But, what then if it is not the artist that makes the idea visual, but someone else? Donald Judd, for one, went to great lengths in 1976 and 1981 in order to claim that such a recreation of one of his pieces of art in actual fact was not art.[244] For Judd, too, the work of art lay not in its manufacturing by the artist or its execution, just as in Conceptual Art, not even entirely in the instruction to those who made it, but – because there would always be a slight difference between the instructions and the executed object – the work became a work of art only through the artist's final *approval*. Presumably this is also the position Duchamp assumed with his many reconstructions. The museums that now harbor those particular objects appear to also hold the same view.

Conceptual Art and Participatory Art, however, are also different in some important ways. One is that Conceptual Art, according to LeWitt, "…is made to engage *the mind* of the viewer rather than his eye or emotions" (my italics). And, furthermore: "It is the objective of the artist who is concerned with Conceptual Art to make his work mentally interesting to the spectator, and therefore usually he would want it to become emotionally dry". In Participatory Art, on the other hand, the artist creates the means by which the spectator can *experience* the multifaceted *emotions* and intellectual challenges inherent in the creative situation. Especially, this applies to the crucial act of executing *choice*. This is so crucial because it is by the spectator's choices that both the work of art and the spectator her/himself comes into being. Conceptual Art is not particularly interested in spectator choice. Participatory Art is made to engage in the spectator the very *emotions* of the creative act and hence also, at best, provide a subjective, emotionally highly significant event.

There are thus highly important differences in the underlying fundamental principles of these two art forms. In particular, there is a difference in how each relates in a very different way to the *spectator*. Conceptual Art produces ideas *to* the spectators. Participatory Art stresses the *involvement* of the spectator through physical *participation* in the creative process, including even the formation of the idea or part of the idea. LeWitt could not have made the ramifications more clear: "When an artist uses a conceptual form of art, it means that all of the planning and decisions are made beforehand (by the artist, my comment) and the execution is a perfunctory affair. The idea becomes *a machine* (my italics) that makes the art. This kind of art is not theoretical or illustrative of theories; it is intuitive, it is involved with all types of mental processes and it is purposeless. It is usually free from the dependence on the skill of the artist as a craftsman". Furthermore "It doesn't really matter if the viewer understands the concepts of the artist by seeing the art."

Another major difference lies in Participatory Art's distinct focus on the actual *carrying out* (and the concurrent subjective experiences) of creating an aesthetic object (but not in the manufacturing of its parts). Whereas: "In Conceptual Art the very *idea* of the concept is the most important aspect of the work" and "...the execution becomes a perfunctory affair. The idea becomes *a machine that makes art*" (my italics), as LeWitt put it.[245] The roles of the "spectator" in each of these two art forms appear to be very different, though they have in common that in both cases they ascribe a different kind of role to the spectator, compared with traditional (retinal) art. In this sense, Participatory Art wants to offer the spectator exactly the opposite of Conceptual Art – a chance to experience the *non-machine* like qualities of human creativity!

How can we sum up a discussion with as many interwoven strands as this one? Some of the elements crucial to Participatory Art can be found in some kinds of paintings and photography, too. Notably, the particular interest is in *the very process of the art work coming into being* as well as the notion of a work of art built up of *several separate elements*. In the world of painting and photography, as well as in Conceptual Art, for a long time, we have seen an ongoing debate about *the possible interest/value or lack of interest/value inherent in a work of art being the original work of art, rather than a copy, or even in the material expression itself*. The very *idea* behind a work of art has been of fundamental interest/value, rather than its manufacturing/execution. This, again, touches upon the auteur-ship of the artist. Conceptual Art stressed the subjective experience and hence also *intuition,* as does Participatory Art.

PART V

POTENTIALS AND PITFALLS FOR THE FUTURE

The limits of ground-breaking artists and the expert artist

Toward the end of the 20th century, few of the artists who earlier at some time or other had worked with something in the vein of Participatory Art were still doing it. The same was still true at the beginning of the 21st century, when Scott McNealy published his article that declared a "Welcome to the Participation age".

Art history seems full of discussions why art evolved this way or that way at the time it did. Less often the question raised is why art did *not* evolve in this way or that way and/or earlier than it, later, did. In fact, I cannot recall having seen any such study.

More specifically, it would be interesting to examine more in depth why some artists, who at the time seemed to come close to develop Participatory Art, did not do so, but rather shied away after some preliminary contact. Even though Participatory Art and abstract art are two different kinds of art, something similar could be said about those artists who came close to focusing on abstract painting, but then in the end refrained from proceeding any further in that direction. Turner is one obvious example.

William Turner, during the first half of the 19th century, broke new ground in painting. In many of his paintings, particularly towards the end of his life, he made a number of semi-abstract paintings, especially in water color. Yet, he did not change his path and go entirely into abstract art. Why did he not? Reading about his life and art gives us few clues. If I should venture a guess, it would be that during his entire life he had been stretching the art of painting as far as the market was prepared to follow, so he knew very well where the limits were. Being financially dependent on selling his art, he could not afford to go beyond what the market could bear. Another explanation might be that we have misunderstood the late Turner. What we know about his late period is based on what was found in his studio after his death. So there is a possibility that what we now consider semi-abstract or fully abstract paintings were unfinished paintings and water color sketches left unfinished at the time of his death.

As has been mentioned earlier, Henri Matisse is another painter who came close to abstraction a few times, especially in the last decade of his life (Matisse died in 1954 at the age of 84). Abstraction appears to be most evident in his gouaches and cut-outs (not least the huge *l'Éscargot* from 1953), and in his maquettes for glass windows. The first time Matisse came close to painting abstract was possibly with *Vue de la Collioure (1905)* or with *Vue de*

Notre Dame (1914), *Le Rideau Jaune* (1914-15) and in particular *Porte-fenêtre à Collioure* (1914).[246] The latter is "The most mysterious painting Matisse ever painted" according to Louis Aragon.[247] Why then did Matisse not proceed into abstract art? Again, it seems we can only surmise: perhaps he had already struggled enough in order to move his painting into the area that eventually became so unmistakably his own, i.e. part of his identity?

"The creators of a new language are always fifty years ahead of their time", Matisse is quoted saying, towards the end of his life.[248] Perhaps he already realized this at the time he made his first semi-abstract painting? Maybe he realized already then that if he pursued this new direction he may not ever become a recognized painter. Perhaps he had already had enough of that and not yet enough of recognition for the highly important changes he had brought to art, so far? Or maybe he just felt he had not yet delved deeply enough into his personal direction?

But perhaps Matisse also doubted the value of making what may have felt like enormous struggles to paint in yet another new way? To Matisse, struggle in itself was not an indicator of the value of a certain direction. "He [Matisse] said he had been mistaken all his life in measuring the significance of any given work by the struggles that went into it."[249]

Georges Braque, during his Cubism years around 1910, came close to producing abstract art, yet he never really became an abstract painter. Why did he not move into abstraction? After all, he had broken radically new ground together with Picasso, in pioneering Cubism. Maybe he was just genuinely contented with this breakthrough? Would not most artists have been satisfied? Or, maybe in Cubism, he had found the personal idiom that suited him best? Or, maybe he was not a forceful enough painter?

Pablo Picasso, contrary to both Matisse and Braque, did reinvent himself several times during his life, when, each time, he left one of his "periods" for something new. Yet, he never moved into an abstract period despite being an otherwise radically innovative painter. Maybe it simply did not fit in with his personality or with his interests in painting?

At least the latter three of the four painters mentioned above could all be said to be pioneers of the Modern Movement in Art even though they did not venture into abstract painting. Three other painters – Kandinsky, Malevitch and Mondrian – were also pioneers of the Modern Movement, but precisely *because* they pioneered abstract painting, even though they had begun their careers more or less as figurative painters. What made those three pioneers of abstract painting? Maybe what they wished to communicate could not be communicated in figurative painting, whilst what Matisse, Braque and Picasso wished to communicate could be better communicated in figurative painting? Could it be that a need to communicate something hitherto un-communicable launched a new form of art? If we accept that argument, then it is also reasonable to assume that the need to communicate through Participatory Art would not have made itself widely felt before the age of Participation had arrived.

Duchamp, another pioneer of the Modern Movement, also created some semi-abstract art. He certainly wanted to overturn the art world when, for example, he put a bicycle wheel or a urinal in an art exhibition (in 1915) claiming that whatever you say is art, is art. But he did not want to open up the art world of the artist, by breaking the barrier between the artist and the spectator. He seems to have made the effort once with the instructions sent to his sister Suzanne in 1916[250] asking her to add her own words to one of his ready-mades, as mentioned above. But he did not pursue this track. Duchamp could easily have developed into an abstract painter, sculptor, or even the first "full time" Participatory Art artist, yet he did not. Instead, in 1923, he went silent. It seems his interests did not lie in abstract painting and he did not seem open to the full potentials of participation in art. Perhaps his perception of the human being prevented him. He certainly seemed to have a more elitist orientation than, for example, Beuys.

Apart from those painters who nearly went into abstract art, but in the end did not do so, there were a few artists who in a similar ways came close to Participatory Art yet did not choose that direction wholeheartedly.

As we have mentioned earlier, Moholy-Nagy became interested in the potentials of participation in art in the 1930s. My guess is that this move was influenced by his background in the Bauhaus School, with its more egalitarian view of mankind and its interest in experimentation. Moholy-Nagy made a few Participatory Art objects in the 1930s, but they had more the character of experiments, and Moholy-Nagy did not pursue the path any further. Perhaps he came to his early experiments in Participatory Art too late in life? His many changes of domicile between the wars probably were not conducive to assuming a more spectacular pioneering role than he actually did. WW II entailed a lot of personal changes and artistic digressions that led him more in the direction of design and writing (he began *Vision in Motion* in 1943 and *Abstract of an Artist* in 1944. He died in 1946).

If we look at the post-WW II years, Joseph Beuys seemed the perfect candidate to develop Participatory Art. Beuys was co-founder of the Fluxus movement in 1962. With his fundamental regard of his pupils and listeners as his equals, and with his oft repeated statement "Everyone is an artist,"[251] it would seem natural for him to create Participatory Art. To the *Information-Action* at the Tate Gallery in 1972, he sent the message "People, you have the power to free yourselves!"[252] "The nature of my sculptures is not fixed and definitive [...]. Everything is in a state of change"[253] Beuys is quoted having said, and his sculptures/installations bear witness of it. Beuys in fact also created the concept of Social Sculpture[254]. He even went so far as to claim that "he would undertake 'a metamorphosis in the concept of art…an anthropology of art'".[255] "The only kind of science that was acceptable to him is that in which a kind of free-form laboratory full of possibilities without solutions is given. 'Chaos can have a healing character,' he [Beuys] said, and so he preached change of all kinds." [256] "My sculpture is not fixed and finished. Processes continue in most of them: chemical reactions, fermentations, color changes, decay, drying up. Everything is in a state of change."[257]

Yet, Beuys, too, stopped short of Participatory Art. Why? Was all his rhetoric just a compensation, even a cover, for the opposite in his strivings – his very didactic drive casting him in the role of teacher-preacher-shepherd-redeemer, of talking *to* his students and to the rest of the world? "No artist ever lectured so much as Beuys"... Borer claims.[258]

In his essay in the catalogue to the 2005 exhibition of Beuys' art at the Tate Modern, Sean Rainbird has explored the "openness of some of Beuys' sculptures, notably with *Tram Stop (1976), The End of the Twentieth Century (1983-85).* Of the latter, Rainbird writes that ""Beuys appears to have stipulated few parameters for the display of the sculpture" and "The range of different installations of this work created by Beuys suggests that there is some flexibility in considering how, even without the artist's personal intervention or in the absence of explicit instructions, someone else can install the sculpture."[259] Note, however, that the aim of the whole effort of the installation at the Tate and elsewhere was to create something that the curators thought might look like something Beuys could have done himself, that is "emulating the artist". This is quite the opposite of Participatory Art, where the aim and to some extent the measure of success, would be to create something that the artist had *not* thought of! Was it really Beuys' intention that the curators should feel so restricted? How does that match his dictum that everyone is an artist? "During his lifetime, Beuys treated his exhibitions as flexible propositions, and treated each opportunity to exhibit his work as a dynamic interaction between artist, object, and space"[260] Note, however, the conspicuous lack of role for the spectator... Except for curators!

Whether he intended it or not, Beuys continued to present a problem to the world even after his death in 1986.

The British sculptor Antony Gormley (born in 1950), among other great achievements, played a central role in reviving monumental sculpture towards the end of the 20th century, through his variables (*Fields* 1991 and subsequent variations), *Critical Man* (1998), and – variable by nature - "*Another Place*" (1997). Gormley is an artist who, as I see it, over a long time moved in the direction of Participatory Art, but only at the beginning of the new millennium has he created major works where the creativity of "the spectator" is one central element of the work. Most notable is probably his sculpture *One and Other* in Trafalgar Square, displayed in the summer of 2009. On a monumental plinth, 2,400 selected "spectators" could take turns for one hour each, being whatever "sculpture" they wished to "perform". If this was monumental performance or monumental Participatory Art, is debatable, however.

A variation on something like Participatory Art, in this case sculpture, is Antony Gormley's now classic *Field for the British Isles* (1993) first version made in Brazil 1991)[261]. In order to create this piece of art, Gormley asked teams of volunteers in Humberside to shape with their hands as many simple figures, as they could, during a couple of days. The figures were based on the same idea. The sunk-in eyes, made by sticking pencils into the clay, gave the figures a ghostlike character. Seen standing "shoulder to shoulder" looking in the same direction (at the spectator) the 40,000 figures or so made a peculiarly dense impression on the spectator. Despite how it came into being, Gormley's conceived idea that the entire installation be viewed from a single viewpoint – the one where all the figures were looking at the spectator – made this installation less of a Participatory Art work. Also, the spectators were neither involved in the assembling of the complete work of art, nor were they invited to re-arrange the parts at will, as far as I know.

In his South Bank Centre exhibition in 2007, Gormley showed a huge glass room filled with steam, lit up in a special way. Spectators could enter this glass room. From outside the glass room they could be seen as parts of moving hominid shadows as they approached or moved along the glass walls. In this case the artistic experience could arguably be said to belong to those watching from the outside. They could of course change roles, enter the glass room and become part of the installation. Was the artist at all interested in how the spectators used their creativity? Could they themselves see any results of their own creativity? Probably not. This is what makes it an installation, perhaps even a somewhat participatory installation, and not an example of Participatory Art.

In 2009 Gormley also exhibited *The Collective Body* which was about how 100 tons of clay in the shape of a block measuring 4 by 4 by 2.6 meters was transformed over a number of days by people aged 8 and over, being invited make their own creations with the clay. The point was the question "can we shift from the obsession with the development of objects … to activity" … "to the fact that we are all makers?"[262] In this piece, the borderline between art and play appears a bit problematic, but not necessarily out of bounds from a Participatory Art point of view. However, the intention of the artist needs to be explained.

Along with these exhibitions, in 2009, Gormley held other exhibitions with much less, if any, participatory angle. Even so, in 2009[263] he stated in a radio interview that "participation is the most important thing that has happened in art." I know of no other artist who has been that explicit. In the same interview, Gormley, in speaking of art and the role of art also said: "Art is a way in which life expresses its own vitality" and "Participation in art is a necessary part of being alive."

Nevertheless, Gormley is not working only with participation in mind. Also in 2009, he held other exhibitions that seemed more like installations or even more traditional sculptures, albeit in radically new form.

All of these artists were well positioned to pioneering Participatory Art, yet none of them did. Why, we do not know. Like with many excellent corporate strategies[264] this may perhaps have less to do with Participatory Art as such, rather than timing. After all, it was not until 2005 that Scott McNealy called out a "Welcome to the Participation age"![265]

Participatory Art around the turn of the millennium

The mood around the turn of the millennium was once again that of a crisis. Paul Greenalgh summed it up thus in 2005: "...a common critique of the current state of things points to the crises in the arts being caused by fragmentation of culture. Modern conditions seems to have undermined the consistency of existence to the point where it can no longer generate a cultural fabric that has any form, depth or longevity; it is as if we live in a cacophony of a million competing and arbitrary sound-bites, DVD clips and internet connections; that we have created a universe in which we have fabricated millions of beads, but have had the thread taken away from us." [266]

It seems to me, that in a society like this, the talent to (re)assemble fragments, i.e. *to create* – preferably instantaneously – will be a crucial talent.

The concept of Interactive Art crops up, but by and large it seems to mean only the possibility of an exchange with the work of art – like setting it in motion, typing on a keyboard or some fanciful activity – but not necessarily a "spectator" participation in a previous initiative to create something. As in "Relational Art" the emphasis seems to be more on some kind of exchange with the art work, rather than on enhancing the creativity of the spectator. Participatory Art is also not the same as co-creating. To me, co-creating means starting from scratch in a joint initiative. In Participatory Art, the artist has already made an artistic initiative and then invites the spectator to leave the classical, fairly passive spectator role and build on – or with - what the artist has initiated. The Participatory Art-work is thus not completely open-ended and there is a defined role for both the artist and the "spectator". Thus the Participatory Art-work is restricted – but only partially restricted – by the original initiative taken by the artist.

The word "participation" has been associated in Germany with Mitbestimmung, (letting employees having a say on company boards, now on the vane at the beginning the 21st century). In France, in March 2005, "participation" was very much in the headlines, but here it meant the partaking in company profits by the salaried workers, rather than the money solely being transferred to shareholders and management (in the shape of bonuses). In the French presidential elections in 2007 the French word "participation" - but now in the more inclusive sense of allowing for everybody to take an active part in the election process and the formulation of policy - became the key mantra to one of the candidates, Ségolène Royal.

In the foreword to his book "Relational Aesthetics "(originally published in French in 1998[267]), art critic Nicolas Bourriaud asked the question "what are the real challenges of contemporary art?" The back cover of the book featured the question: "Where does our current obsession for interactivity stem from?" The material in between these two questions is a book that emphasizes the interest of some contemporary art in involving the spectator in new ways, emphasizing the relationship be-tween the spectator and the work of art. Judging from the examples of works of art that Bourriaud described, the Cuban born American Gonzales-Torres being the prime example, this relationship can be of many kinds, some of them more participatory than other. What they have in common, however, is the emphasis put on *the relation itself,* rather than on the creativity of the spectator. Just as earlier Environments, Happenings, and so on, also tried to bridge the gap between artist and public, these seem to be primarily social experiments focusing on *interactivity as such,* not necessarily challenging the creativity of the individual. The relations explored seem to be more as an alternative to the relationship consumer – products that otherwise seems so prevalent in contemporary society, even affecting social relations.

In fact, the definition Bourriaud made of Relational Art was that it is "an art taking as its theoretical horizon the realm of human interactions and its social context, rather than the assertion of an independent and *private* symbolic space."[268] This is a far cry from focusing on the creativity of the spectator and for that reason inviting the spectator to leave the relative passivity inherent in that role. Yet, participation is of interest also to Bourriaud, but more as a "system of intensive encounters" – "an art form where the substrate is formed by inter-subjectivity, and which takes *being-together* (my italics) as the central theme, the 'encounter' between holder and picture, and the collective elaboration of meaning."[269]

As we are talking about tendencies towards Participatory Art around the turn of the millennium, I think it is important in this context to also mention the Danish/Icelandic artist Olafur Eliasson (born 1967); not because of his extraordinary, successful installation *The Weather Project* at the Tate Modern, London, in 2003 – over 2.2 million visitors came to see it – but because Eliasson is profoundly interested in interaction with the spectators. Already at the Kunstakademiet, towards the end of the 1980s, he began to "explore how the subject might become co-producer or a constituent of a work of art"[270] (my translation from Danish). "My concern is 'How can I set up a practice of having people interacting with the work in a way that doesn't formalize the process into telling them what to experience? How can the piece constantly change with the people coming in? How can the piece one day be like this and the next day be something else?' And in order to leave the openness in the piece it's very important not to lock up in a certain frame that tells people how to see it."[271] Eliasson's emphasis in his work, however, seems to be more on building a relation with the audience, however, than bringing something out of the individual spectator. Eliasson's kind of spectator involvement so far seems to be perhaps more in line with the ideomotoric movements we saw already with Duchamp[272] and again in the 1950s and 1960s, rather than on the actual individual creativity of the spectator. On the individual level, Eliassson's stated intention is "... to get the participants to see themselves sensing."[273] (My translation from Danish). The intention, certainly, is to activate them, but not necessarily to help them experience their own creativity.

In the summer of 2007 the exhibition *Reconstruction 2* was held at Sudeley Castle in Gloucestershire, UK. Among those exhibiting were the Mexican installation and performance artist Carlos Amorales with his "Exotic Raven". This piece, called "a participatory work" by Richard Cork, art critic in the Financial Times, was described as "a jumbo-size jigsaw puzzle" in multicolored, highly reflective paint, radiating outwards and spreading across a terrace, tempting the spectator to grab the pieces and "push them round in different configurations".[274] This sounds like something in the vein of Participatory Art work, though no mention is made of the spectator's creativity, nor if there is a point in having the spectator "push them round" the separate pieces "in different configurations" other than just amusement. This illustrates, I believe, the dangers for Participatory Art, if it were to continue without any theoretical foundation. It runs the risk of being reduced to entertainment only.

Also in the summer of 2007, in the Documenta exhibition in Kassel, two works of art with participatory elements were on display. The scope for participation from the spectator was rather limited, once again. The Brasilian artist, curator and author Ricardo Basbaum had developed something called "a communicative framework to enable the circulation of actions and forms. With diagrams, drawings, texts and installations he creates interactions in which the individual personal experience of the actors and viewers participating reveals an essential quality." The name of this installation was *Would you like to participate in an artistic experience? (1994-2007)*. The installation may also be experienced – at least partly - at www.nbp.pro.br. [275] The other work in a participatory vein was a kind of installation by the Chilean Gonzalo Diaz called *Eclipses*. From a purely technical point of view, this work of art basically consists of a "cuboid-shaped installation, profile spotlight and text panel". The spectator is asked "to stand in the way of a beam of light so that their shadow falls on the inscription on a small panel making it legible."[276] But how much room was there for the creativity of the spectator?

If the above-mentioned works of art by Carlos Amorales, Ricardo Basbaum and Gonzalo Dias are somewhat representative of art with a participatory aspect to them, then it is of interest to notice how relatively little they deliberately engage the creativity of the spectator. From that point of view, not much seems to have happened since the early decades of the 20th century. In fact, from the particular point of view of spectator participation, the works by Charlotte Posenenske from 1967, also on show at this Documenta, in some ways represent a further development. This lack of development direction, I believe, is exactly what can be expected in a field of art without a well developed theory behind it. The art is moving in circles rather than gaining new ground. It is high time to formulate a theory or agenda of Participatory Art!

Art in the age of non-reproduction.

The sentence above is, of course, a take-off on Walter Benjamin's classical 1936 essay "The Work of Art in the Age of Mechanical Reproduction". Benjamin was talking about art in the age of mass production. Increasingly, our own age is leaving mass production and its co-committant, mass marketing, behind. We are now in an age where marketing to one is the guiding principle. The car maker BMW boasts that they can manufacture 750,000 varieties of their cars. For that to be meaningful, the company needs the customer's input – a form of participation – in order to tailor the final model to the customer's wish. Participatory Art also needs the customer's input to come into being. *But, to Participatory Art, reproduction is not a meaningful concept. Instead, the experience of participating in the creation as such is the core product. That experience, unlike the ensuing result, can not be reproduced in any meaningful way.* In this sense, Participatory Art has been long awaiting the demise of Walter Benjamin's Age of Mechanical Reproduction and the advent of the Participation age that Scott McNealy proclaimed in 2005 (quoted at the beginning of this essay).

Meanwhile, I find it intriguing, that the beginnings of a new movement in art has slowly unfolded for nearly 100 years, without really taking off as a distinct movement of its own, when so many other revolutions have taken place within modern art during this same period.

Part of the answer is probably that the art market complex – galleries-collectors-museums etc.) has been geared to the unique object as the only one with an investment potential. The art market has not been primarily dedicated to spectator experiences focused on their own creativity.[277] In fact, during the 1960s, there was a strong tendency amongst artists to try to distance their art from the institutions of the art world and its dictums, as we have seen with Lygia Clark, Charlotte Posenenske, Joseph Beuys, Multiples etc.

Participatory, yes – but is it art?

All that involves the spectator in an activity of color, line and shape, clearly is not Participatory Art. Not even if it includes a large element of chance. See for example http://www.ipollock.com/ where the internet user can play around with doodling vaguely reminding one of Pollock's techniques.

The question whether Participatory Art is art or not is not simply a seemingly eternal academic question. The question is being asked here in order to help us understand why the many fundamentals of Participatory

Art, resurfacing again in the 1950s and 1960s, did not lead to a steady growth, let alone an explosion, of this kind of art.

From what has been said in the preceding chapters, it is clearly impossible to give a final answer to the question whether Participatory Art is or is not art, as it depends on what criteria for art is used. A reasonable way out of this dilemma is to state that Participatory Art definitely is a *kind of* art, just like Minimal Art or Conceptual Art, although not as circumscribed. But it is not a kind of art that fits in snuggly with the art market (and hence has problems fitting in with the various parts of the "signature artist"-critic-collector-art fair-auction room-museum-complex). An issue that is yet to be settled is if an immediately recognizable signature style is possible for an artist working with Participatory Art. Personally I believe it is. We do not yet, however, have the necessary overview of the entire field, in order to settle this issue. Not so long ago, beauty and harmony were the only legitimate foci for art. At other times, human perception, reality, even horror (as with Goya), and ugliness were legitimate foci for art. Strangely enough, never before has human creativity as such, as a process in itself worthy of artistic exploration, been the major focus of any art; and certainly not the creativity of the spectators! Nor has the experience of the creative moment as it unfolds been thoroughly explored. As long as Participatory Art sticks to those two foci, I believe also this kind of art will have a role to play.

What is art, anyway? Denise René defined what Stefan Germer described as "the Iron Law of the art market".

This states that "For something to be sold as art it has to be recognized as art." Germer continued, "as long as it, beyond doubt, is not possible to identify a piece of work as art, because of the techniques and the materials used, then its identity as a work of art must be ascertained through other established means of guarantee, like for example the name of its maker, place of exhibition, origin, price, and to a limited extent, expert opinion." [278] (My translation from German.)

It is worthwhile here to dwell a moment on the commercial problems that Multi Art encountered. They may explain not only the demise of Multi Art after its revival in the early 1980s, but also the difficulties encountered by Participatory Art – and the ultimate explanation why Participatory Art never took off in the 1950s and 1960s, despite the success of the exhibition "Le movement" at Galerie Denise René in 1955 and the first Edition MAT in 1959/60.

Fundamental in ascertaining the value of a work of art in those days was the role played by the art market – basically the whole gallery-critic-collector-auction room-museum-complex. The major problem for this complex when encountering Multi Art (and in all likelihood also Participatory Art) was to ascertain whether a creation was a unique art object or one in a series of identical objects, or a mere reproduction, or indeed if the creation had anything to do with art at all, rather than being just a gadget, a game, a toy (like Lego), a piece of design or simply a piece of interior decoration (like candlestick holders or fit-together shelves). In 2007, however, the Danish-Icelandic artist Olafur Eliasson exhibited tables with Lego pieces for people to assemble, on one of the main squares in Copenhagen. But all the Lego pieces were in white…

To make things worse, the struggle to ascertain if an object was a piece of art was countered by several artists – with very different views amongst themselves – struggling against this process. Notable positions were taken by Andy Warhol and Joseph Beuys and later also Donald Judd as well as Sol Le Witt. The same flowers by Warhol printed on canvas, paper, or as posters fetched very different prices. Warhol's Brillo Boxes keep on causing a debate about what is authentic and not.

At the heart of the problem was the fact that with a lot of modern art – from Duchamp's Ready-mades, via Jean Fautrier's experimental paintings in 1949-1954 and Multi Art, to Minimalists like Donald Judd, Carl Andre, and Sol LeWitt – there were no originals to begin with and hence there could be no copies. These art objects were either made in an open series where – unlike etchings – no one number in the whole series could be suspected of being of better or of worse quality. Sometimes there was not even a series of objects, but just the instructions for how to make them and sometimes also samples. Sometimes the specific site was claimed as part of the art work, sometimes not.

Some artists would refuse the right of reproduction of their works without the artist's authorization; on grounds that only the artist could decide what was an authentic work by him (Andre). Judd took a slightly different stand claiming that it is impossible to know exactly how a piece of art would turn out from the instructions and therefore the artist's approval of each work was a sine qua non for the work to be considered a piece of art by him.

LeWitt, on the other hand, compared his instructions for wall paintings to sheets of music that were performed in various places and at various times with none being an original more than another. Robert Morris drew comparisons with photography and claimed that the actual sale of a work of art was the defining moment for what was art and what was not art.

By the standards of Judd or Andre, I suppose bronze castings made posthumously from Rhodin or Giacometti sculptures should not be considered original works of art rather than mere copies – a position I doubt the art market would unreservedly support. With the definitions of either LeWitt or Morris, the issue of distinguishing a fake from an original – a key concept in the art market – becomes very problematic. Encouragingly, this shows that art – as opposed to art objects – does not let itself be defined by the art market alone.

Is there a need for Participatory Art?

Öyvind Fahlström pointed out that "*Without manipulating the work of art you do not realize the fantastic nature of the astronomical freedom of choice...*"[279] (My italics). But is there really a demand from the public for an "astronomical freedom of choice"? With choice also comes the inherent responsibility for choosing. Are we always prepared to assume this responsibility? In the moment of choice we become responsible not only for the end result, but also for our own identity.[280] Do we really want to dwell on that in a deliberate and contemplated manner? Or, do we prefer to take our identities for granted or as givens?

On the other hand, the usage of the words "interactive" and "participatory" has been on a steady increase in various areas of society during the past few decades. Then, is this not a natural field for art to explore, just as art previously explored light, space, color, machines, movement, and so on?

A final argument for the need for Participatory Art is that traditional, finished art – unlike Participatory Art - can not adequately convey or reflect the unfolding character of the creative *process*. Just like the surrealists found that the medium of film better expressed "the temporal or unfolding nature of dreams" than traditional painting did, Participatory Art can express the great variety of emotions that enter into the creative moment.

It could be said that we are now living in *the age of Process*, when all large-scale production more and more is focusing on the very process of production, thus emulating the phenomenal success of the production model developed by Toyota, replacing the classical mass production model developed by Ford and GM in the 1920s.[281] Incidentally, the Toyota model stresses full *participation* and individual responsibility by all workers.[282]

What then holds back the development of Participatory Art?

The critic and scholar Jean-Francois Chevrier indirectly touches upon this issue when he described what happened with a few of the participatory objects that were exhibited at the 1961 exhibition Movement in Art – Rörelse i Konsten – in Stockholm: "The actions by which Kaprow and Rauschenberg invited the viewer to create (or complete) the work of art were too complicated and unconventional for most people. They only stimulated protest actions or froze the viewer in shyness. Tinguely and Stankiewicz stayed at the level of the average viewer – the viewer's action was as simple as the usual 'make-into-art" action: looking. At the same time it was activating by making the viewer feel like *a co- creator also in the physical sense.*"[283] Kaprow and Rauschenberg were concrete/abstract in asking people to take part in open-ended works of art, by using material provided and with no specific result specified. Tinguely and Stankiewicz only asked the spectators to operate machines they had designed themselves. The difference, I believe, is exactly between making the spectator *"feel like a co-creator"* in some kind of interactivity sense, rather than make the spectator actually experience – even if only for a short moment – her or his own creativity.

Judging from Chevrier's words above, one may conclude that one factor that has held back the development of Participatory Art has been the *complexity of the demand it puts on the "spectator"*. This may be true, but it may also be a matter of how this form of art is presented

Other obstacles to the development of Participatory Art may be simple practical details such as how one can exhibit Participatory Art, when so many people tend to walk away with whatever is not fastened or behind glass, everything they can lay their hands on? Art critic Guy Brett suggested this as an explanation of why an artist like Lygia Clark has been so relatively little known. Suely Rolnik also pointed out this problem when preparing for the exhibition of Clark in Nantes.

A more sinister explanation may be found within Participatory Art itself. Did Lygia Clark and Öyvind Fahlström as well as Charlotte Posenenske express themselves though something in the vein of Partici-patory Art because that kind of art fitted best with their inner worlds and perhaps also with some less well integrated traumas? Or did their explorations in the direction of Participatory Art cause them stress and strain (two moved away from art and all three died prematurely), and in that case why would this be so, and could this be a factor that keeps other artist away? Artists working in a Participatory Art vein have to a large extent been working in a vacuum. All through the latter part of the 20th century there was a total lack of interest in this kind of art. But inherent in Participatory Art is also a lack of personal recognition in that the work of art per definition is never completed without someone else taking part. So, in order to work with Participatory Art, the artist needs to be emotionally quite independent. Both financially and in terms of personal recognition, the rewards need to come from somewhere else than from the artistic activity alone. This has probably not encouraged the development of Participatory Art.

A more banal explanation for why Participatory Art, so far, has never really taken off, despite so many roots developing during such a long time, could, of course also be that the public has not seen anything it likes and therefore not encouraged such art. Fahlström, for example, with his strong interest in geo-politics and being very much a provocateur, would probably not fit in with the buying interests of many people at the time. Could it be that Participatory Art does not lend itself very well to painting? As Chevrier put it in the book on Fahlström: "The price of freedom was an impoverishment of painting, a renunciation of the substantial richness of the pictorial medium. To gain a greater mobility, the figures had to be reduced to cut-outs, like silhouettes against a depthless ground."[284] Perhaps this was not attractive to the art-loving public? Or, perhaps this would not be true for abstract painting? Can we imagine artists like Arp, Matisse (while doing cut outs), or Miro making variable paintings? Would something important in their art have been lost? Calder did try variable paintings, but settled for mobile sculpture, instead. Could it be that Participatory Art lends itself more to sculpture than to painting?

Possible ways forward – the theories of Mondrian

Chevrier, in the book on Fahlström, suggests that one way forward for the kind of interactive art that Fahlström made – and perhaps this is also applicable to Participatory Art – would be to appeal to the human instinct for play and games; and another way would be to build on the element of instruction. "If the viewer can discover a fascination with 'playing' with objects, he might also learn to play with forms, signs structures in in Mobile Artworks – i.e., become *a co-creator in his experience* in a rich and active way."[285] At least Fahlström had already responded to this suggestion, when he said in an interview with Lazlo Gloser, in 1974: "If I were only, or mainly, interested in educating the viewers, I would create simpler structures, and use other media than hand-made art. I see myself as a witness, rather than an educator."[286] It is also important here to differentiate between participating in the making of a static work of art and participating in the experiences of making open works of art. Maybe the solution lies in using simpler structures.

It seems to me that, underlying art today, there are two different assumptions about the nature of art. On the one hand you find Duchamp's, in my opinion rather superficial dictum, that "Art is a game between all people of all periods"[287] with its implied distancing from the actual creativity of the artist. On the other hand you can find a more profound view of the artist as an explorer of reality or perhaps even of realities, or parts of either. The exploration of games is, of course, also an exploration, albeit a limited one, just like the exploration of relations in modern relational art. Exploring creativity seems to me a wider, more profound, and more meaningful exploration to make.

I believe that Participatory Art to some extent appeals to the spectator's playfulness, which is no mean feat. "… On the basis of playing is built the whole of man's experiential existence" wrote the famous psychoanalyst and child psychologist Donald Winnicott.[288] I also believe that there is an educational element in Participatory Art beyond that of other visual arts. "…It is only in being creative that the individual discovers the self."[289] Psychological theory supports this statement, to some extent.

While the above seems true enough to me, to make it the sole foundation of Participatory Art would be to unnecessarily denigrate or devalue Participatory Art as a kind of art in its own right. It is better then to try to develop a theory of Participatory Art, in order to understand this kind of art better, and in doing so, connect the theory to other theoretical works on art that are relevant to Participatory Art.

Two such theoretical contributions of relevance to Participatory Art are Piet Mondrian's essay *Plastic Art and Pure Plastic Art* (1937) and Umberto Eco's *L'Oeuvre ouverte* (*Opera Aperta* 1962).

Umberto Eco tried in his book to describe a "dialectic between form and 'openness', between free *multi-polarity* and the permanence of the *work* even in the variety of its many possible readings.[290] "Umberto Eco attempted to define the 'open work' beyond the simple idea that any work can be the object of multiple interpretations. He described works, particularly of music and literature (especially Ulysses and Finnegan's Wake by James Joyce, my comment), which were open in their very structure, in a combinatory mode that incorporated chance. He spoke of works founded on 'the recognition that the world is a knot of possibilities'[291]" In the fifth chapter of his book, however, Eco then also said that "Life is not 'openness' but chance. To transform this chance *into a knot of possibilities*, it is necessary to introduce an organizational schema. *One must choose* the elements of a constellation, among which one can then – but only then – establish polyvalent relationships"[292] (My italics). To this I would add what Eco suggests in the sixth chapter, under the heading of *The poetics of the Open work*: "Order has become the simultaneous presence of diverse orders. It is up to each reader to choose his own" (my translation). In my mind, what Eco here says could equally well refer to Participatory Art.

Mondrian, on the other hand, already in the second

paragraph of his essay *Plastic Art and Pure Plastic Art* (1937), tells us that "Throughout the history of culture, art has demonstrated that universal beauty does not arise from the particular character of the form, but from the *dynamic rhythm of its inherent relationships*, or – in a composition – from *the mutual relations of forms*. Art has shown that it *is a question of determining these relations*. It has revealed that the forms exist only for the creation of relationships; that forms create relations and that relations create forms. In this duality of forms and their relations neither takes precedence."[293](My italics) Mondrian also writes that "For pure art then, the subject can never be an additional value; it is the line, the color, and *the relations* which must 'bring into play the whole sensual and intellectual register of inner life…,' not the subject. Both in abstract art and in naturalistic art color express itself 'in accordance with the form, by which it is determined,' and in all art it is the artist's task to make forms and colors living and capable of arousing emotion."[294]

In the same essay, Mondrian furthermore writes that "Nonfigurative art is created by establishing *a dynamic rhythm of determined mutual relations* which *excludes the formation of any particular form*. We note thus, that to destroy particular form is only to do more consistently what all art has done."[295]

Can we from this conclude that Participatory Art, in order to thrive, will need to be a non-figurative art? Does that partially explain why Fahlström's figurative kind of Participatory Art did not break new ground, allowing others to follow suit? I am inclined to think so.

In a passage that is almost pure premonition, Mondrian

then writes: "The less obvious the artist's hand the more objective will the work be. This fact leads to a preference for a more or less mechanical execution or to the materials employed by industry. Hitherto, of course, these materials have been imperfect from the point of view of art. If these materials and their colors were more perfect and if a technique existed by which the artist could easily cut them up in order to compose his work as he conceives it, *an art more real and more objective in relation to life than painting would arise.*"[296] (My italics.)

Mondrian is especially noted for his role in the development of non-figurative art, of which he says that "All art has achieved a certain measure of abstraction" and "this abstraction has become more and more accentuated…"[297] What Mondrian stressed is not play or education, but the use of intuition, creativity and individual expression. "In general, people have not realized that *one can express our very essence through neutral constructive elements*; that is to say, *we can express the essence of art.*"[298] (My italics.)

If we swap the word "art" used in the quotation above from Mondrian for the word "creativity", which, personally, I perceive to be the essence of art, then I believe Mondrian's prophetic sentence applies not only to art in our times but also equally well to organizations and whole societies – thus bridging the age old gap between art and society.

If "life is transformation", as Mondrian put it, then Participatory Art is the kind of art that more than any other kind of art specifically mirrors our times.

At first sight it might seem a bit odd to end this book by turning our attention back to Mondrian. We seem to think that the development of art – like scientific progress – is linear. Art, however, fundamentally deals with human nature and the relationship between human nature and the world it finds itself in. Thus, it might be more fruitful to look at the development of art as a spiral process. Then, it is logical to re-connect with predecessors, but at a different level, with a different perspective than they could possibly have taken. By staying in contact with earlier art movements, art can avoid the traps of temporary fads and fashions and stay true to the eternal tasks of art, which is to explore and enrich what every generation sees as reality, producing material that poses profound questions for us to ask and reflect upon. This book has endeavored to show how a different kind of art – Participatory Art and its various roots during the 20th century – has strived to integrate into art *the creative moment in its unfolding in real time* and therefore also *human creativity in action.* Few phenomena could be more central to art.

PART VI

ON A PERSONAL NOTE

When I first exhibited my own art, at Galleri Händer in Stockholm in 1982, I called my exhibition *Participatory Art (1972-1982)*. I used the term Participatory Art to describe a kind of art that focuses *not* on the end result of the creative process, like a finished painting or a finished sculpture, but on the very heart of art – the process of creating art. How else, but through what I called Participatory Art, could I share what I found so exhilarating in life? And so absolutely essential to mankind! This very heart of art was – and still is – my own personal driving force in my own art.

In my own attempt to make Participatory Art, I also explored what *minimum* fundamentals are necessary for someone else, to experience something as being aesthetically pleasing (rather than just a work of art). This focus on *the bare minimum* is something different from the ground rules laid down by, for example, the Classical system of composition "The Golden Section" or the rules of Paul Klee in his "Contributions to the Teaching of Artistic Forms" (1921-1922). This focus on bare minimums also differs from Kandinsky's "Grammar of Forms" (1926) and his principles laid down in "Analysis of the Primary Elements of Painting" (1928) – essentially "a theory of composition as a grammar of abstract painting", according to Norbert Schmitz[299].

My focus on the bare minimum made me interested in Minimalist Art, although my approach is more in the vein of the British philosopher Richard Wollheim's now famous essay "Minimalism". He wrote it in 1965 without any knowledge of Minimalist artists,[300] other than from the writings of the Minimalist artists themselves. When I started creating Participatory Art, I had no knowledge of any of these texts. But then true art is not made from theories, even less to illustrate theories, but more from undefined needs to make something without a need for it to be useful.

When I had my first solo exhibition in the spring of 1982, Torsten Bergmark, then art critic at the prominent Swedish daily Dagens Nyheter, told me that to his knowledge I was the first artist to be *exclusively working* in the vein Participatory Art; and also the first artist ever to have had his first solo exhibition exclusively based on Participatory Art. How come, I wondered?

One factor that has held back the development of Participatory Art might be the complexity of the demand that Participatory Art puts on the spectator as well as on those exhibiting Participatory Art. This might be true, but it may also be a matter of how this kind of art is presented. In 1993, for example, I took part in a selected exhibition at the Kalmar Konstmuseum in Sweden. There I provided a sketchbook next to the elements of Participatory Art that I exhibited, and encouraged the spectators to draw suggestions for changes to the sculpture. Later in the same day I would execute some of the suggested changes. In just a few days, several sketchbooks were filled.

Another fact may be that Participatory Art does not lend itself so easily to painting or for that matter to photography which, besides being arts in themselves, are also primary ways that knowledge about art is spread.

In my own photography, particularly over the last 10-15 years I have tried to explore a direction that with hindsight is related to Participatory Art in kind. In principle, however, it is not unrelated to the indeterminate pictures from the turn of the last century that Dario Gamboni has so well described and that I have quoted earlier in the text. It is important, however, to differentiate between participating in the making of a static work of art and participating in the experiences of making open works of art.

At the end of the last chapter, I suggested that Participatory Art might progress by turning to simpler structures. This has certainly been my own preferred mode of artistic expression. In my art, I enjoy exploring just how simple the structures can be that make up a piece of Participatory Art[301] or in fact any kind of art.

End Notes

1   Paul Klee: *On Modern Art* Manuscript for a speech given at the Art Museum in Jena 1924.

2   Scott McNealy: *The advantages of the global village.* Article in the Financial Times June 8, 2005.
Sun Microsystems had in 2005 a turnover of more than US $ 11 billion and over 31 000 employees in more than 100 countries.

3   Steve Prentice: *The year ahead: Participation is the latest watchword.* Article in the Financial Times Digital Business Report, 14 December 2005. The Gartner Group was in 2005 the world's largest Information Technology research and advisory company.

4   http://www.wired.com/news/ technology/0,1282,69114,00.html October 6, 2005.

5   More and more major media are featuring more user-generated content. I do not know who first coined the term "participatory journalism", but I first saw it used by Emma Saunders in a Financial Times article on the 31st of December 2007. "Perhaps the rise of participatory journalism should have been among Gideon Rachman's choices of the events that defined 2007…" she wrote.
In the French election campaign 2006/7 the French

presidential candidate Ségolène Royal used the terminology of participation in for instance calling her budget a "budget participatif" and making lots of room both on her website and her presidential campaign for user and voter participation. In the US presidential election in 2008, the Internet played a decisive role for the first time.

Since 1989, an organization has been promoting shared decision making and collaborative care in medicine (http://www.fimdm.org/shared_decision_making.php) and http://www.fimdm.org/bibliography.php#development) Coaches help individuals gain the knowledge and motivation they need to become more meaningful participants in the treatment process. (http://www.healthdialog.com/hd/Core/Background/shareddecisionmaking.htm)

6   Lenny T Mendonca and Robert Sutton: *Succeeding at open-source innovation: an interview with Mozilla's Mitchell Baker*. McKinsey Quarterly. January 2008.

7   Sibyl Moholy-Nagy quoted by Achim Borchardt-Hume in *Two Bauhaus Histories*. Achim Borchardt-Hume:*Albers and Moholy-Nagy. From the Bauhaus to the New World* Tate Publishing 2006 (catalogue to the exhibition), p 74.

8   Piet Mondrian: *The New Plastic in Painting* (1917). Reprinted and translated in the collected writings of Mondrian in Harry Holtzman & Martin S. James (Eds): *The New Art – The New Life. The Collected Writings of Piet Mondrian*. 1986 and reprinted 1993.

9   Quoted in Paul Greenhalgh: *The Modern Ideal* V&A Publications 2005, p 208, without any date given.

10   Piet Mondrian: *The New Art – The New Life: The Culture of Pure Relationships* (1931) Reprinted and translated in the collected writings of Mondrian Harry Holtzman & Martin S. James (Eds): *The New Art – The New Life. The Collected Writings of Piet Mondrian.* 1986 and reprinted 1993.

11   In Stephane Mallarmé's article *The Impressionists and Edouard Manet.* Mentioned in Dario Gamboni: *Potential Images. Ambiguity and Indeterminacy in Modern Art.* Reaktion Books 2002, p 178 and footnote 60, p 280

12   Paul Greenhalgh: *The Modern Ideal* V&A Publications 2005, p 149.

13   Michael Fried: *Art and Objecthood.* Artforum 1997.

14   D.W. Winnicott *Playing and Reality* Routledge 1971.

15   Miwon Kwon: *One Place After Another. Notes on Site Specificity.* October 8. 1997.

16   C.f. Albert Rothenberg: *Creativity – the healthy muse.* Lancet 2006;368:58-59.

17   Piet Mondrian: *Plastic Art and Pure Plastic Art* (1936) Reprinted and translated in he collected writings of Mondrian in Harry Holtzman & Martin S. James (Eds): *The New Art – The New Life. The Collected Writings of Piet Mondrian.* 1986 and reprinted 1993.

18   Piet Mondrian: *The New Art – The New Life: The Culture of Pure Relationships* (1931) Reprinted and translated in he collected writings of Mondrian in Harry Holtzman

& Martin S. James (Eds): *The New Art – The New Life. The Collected Writings of Piet Mondrian*. 1986 and reprinted 1993.

19   Anish Kapoor quoted in: Edward Lucie-Smith: *Sculpture Since 1945*. Phaidon 1987, p 140.

20   W. H. Winnicot: *Playing and Reality* 1971.

21   Catherine Millet: *Conversations avec Denise René*. Adam Biro, Paris 1991, p 77.

22   Paul Greenhalgh: *The Modern Ideal* V&A Publications 2005, p 85.

23   Dario Gamboni: *Potential Images. Ambiguity and Indeterminacy in Modern Art*. Reaktion Books 2002.

24   Dario Gamboni: *Potential Images. Ambiguity and Indeterminacy in Modern Art*. Reaktion Books 2002, p 219.

25   Paul Greenhalgh: *The Modern Ideal*. V&A publications 2005, pp 93, 97.

26   Paul Greenhalgh: *The Modern Ideal*. V&A publications 2005, p 147.

27   … "and 'assemblage' duly became a vogue-word among art critics" according to Edward Lucie-Smith, who also mentions the catalogue to that exhibition, written by William C. Seitz, as being "influential". Edward Lucie-Smith: *Sculpture Since 1945*. Phaidon 1987, p 50.

28   Norbert M. Schmitz: *Teaching by Wassily Kandinsky and Paul Klee* in Jeannine Fiedler (Ed):*Bauhaus*. Köneman 2006 (English edition), p 389.

29   An edited version of this conversation can be found in *Art News*, September 1966. The original conversation took place in a WBAI-FM program called *New Nihilism or New Art?*, where Judd and Stella were interviewed both at the same time by Bruce Glaser.

30   Michael Fried: *Art and Objecthood*. Artforum 1997.

31   Douglas Crimp: *Redifining Site Specificity* in *On the Museum's Ruins*. MIT Press 1993.

32   Michael Fried: *Art and Objecthood*. Artforum 1997 ..."the experience of literalist art is of an object *in a situation* – one that, virtually by definition, *includes the beholder*." (Fried's italics). Fried also quotes Robert Morris writing about the relative importance of the size of the object, saying that: "However, it is just this distance between object and subject that creates a more extended situation, because *physical participation becomes necessary*." (my italics) This quote is taken from Robert Morris: *Notes on Sculpture. Part two*. Artforum October 1966.

33   *Définitions* in Internationale Situationniste no 1, 1958. Various ideas of Guy Debord could have put him on the road to Participatory Art, but led him instead to political involvement. Amongst his many ideas I would like to point out his mapping out of "his" separate parts of Paris – the areas he frequented and had a mental image of - into some kind of collage that reminds one of Öyvind Fahlström's paintings. Debord wished to point out that we all make our own personal collages, "Psychogeographie", of the cities we live in. Debord was also a sharp critic of what he described as the commodity fetishism in contemporary society thus distancing him from the object as the highest value.

34   Marcel Duchamp: *The Creative Act*. End of speech given in 1957 in Houston, Texas and later published in *Art News*, volume 56 no 4, summer 1957 and together with a translation into French by himself i. al. in *Le Processus Créatif*. L'Échoppe 1987.

35   See for example Harel, I. and Papert, S. (Eds) *Constructionism*. Ablex Publ. Corp. Norwood, NJ 1991 and Seymour Papert: *The Children's Machine* Basic Books 1993.

36   Now in the Museum of Modern Art in New York.

37   Arthur C. Danto: *The abuse of beauty*. Daedalus, Fall 2002.

38   Douglas Crimp: *Redefining Site Specificity* in *On the Museum's Ruins*. MIT Press 1993.

39   Interactive art is not synonymus with Participatory Art as the level of interaction in interactive art usually has been very limited, like being asked to push a button etc. The aim is also clearly different.

40   See for example Cezanne's *Rocks and Branches at Bibémus* 1900-1904 which even the art dealer Volard had a hard time deciding where the top was according to Rewald qoted in Gamboni, p 113.

41   See for example parts of the Waterlily Suite in the Jeux de Paume Museeum and some of the 21 paintings in his series from the Seine near Giverny painted 1896-1897.

42   See for example Braque's *The Portuguese* from 1911 (now in Kunstmuseum, Basle) and Picasso's *Ma Jolie* also from 1911 (now in MOMA, New York) both reproduced in Robert Hughes: *The Shock of the New* BBC, London 1980.

43   Wikipedia on Cubism.

44   One of the forefathers of Expressionism, Paul Gauguin, advocated for a style of painting he called Synthesism. Gauguin believed in the use of emotive line and color to depict scenes that were not exactly abstract, but also not drawn directly from nature. He believed that a combination, or synthesis, of impression and the visual elements of line and color would produce a more successful painting. Patterns and large forms in expressive color typify the work of Gauguin and his colleague Émile Bernard. Working within the wake of the Impressionists' absolute faith in color and light, Synthesism pushed this legacy into a more abstract outcome of the possibilities of pigment. They felt that nature would be best reproduced in this manner. The short-lived style was at its height from 1888 to 1894, but was reborn in Art Nouveau, the massive style that enjoyed popularity in Europe and America. Example: Paul Gauguin created the tradition of Synthesism (from http://www.itheo. com/art-styles-periods/art-styles-periods_m-s.html).

45   Paul Greenhalgh: *The Modern Ideal* V&A Publications 2005, p 165.

46   Gauguin in a letter to Émile Schuffenecker in 1888 quoted in Paul Greenhalgh: *The Modern Ideal* V&A Publications 2005, p 165.

47   Dario Gamboni: *Potential Images. Ambiguity and Indeterminacy in Modern Art*. Reaktion Books 2002, p 142.

48   See for example Rainer K. Wick: *Teaching at the Bauhaus*. Hatje Cantz 2000. Chapters 2-3.

49   People like Dewey, Götze, Itten (in particular),

Kerschensteiner for example. See Rainer K. Wick: *Teaching at the Bauhaus.* Hatje Cantz 2000. Chapter 5.

50   Ulf Linde: *Marcel Duchamp.* Rabén & Sjögren 1986. Årsbok för Statens Konstmuseer 32, p 115 my translation of Linde's translation into Swedish.

51   My translation from the Swedish text *Kort framställning av rörelsekonstens historia under 1900-talet av K.G. Hultén* in the catalogue to the exhibition of Kinetic Art at the Moderna Museet in Stockholm 17 May – 3 September 1961.

52   I am here thinking of : *Méchanique de la pudeur, pudeur méchanique* (1912), the oil painting *La Mariée...* (1912), *Broyeuse de chocolat no 1 (*Chocolate Grinder no 1*)* (1913) and *Chocolate Grinder no 2* (1914), *3 stoppages étalon* (Three Standard Stoppages) (1913-14), *Glissière contenant un Moulin à eau en métaux voisin* (1913-15) and *Neuf moules malice* (1914-15).

53   His notes and sketches of details to *La Mariée...* were published in 1934 in a small facsimile edition bearing the same name as the big glass painting *La Mariée...*, but usually called *La Boite Verte (The Green Box).* A few more notes on *La Mariée...* were found after Duchamp's death in 1968 and were published in *Notes* in 1980.

54   Lest the reader should find this argument far fetched let us remember that those were the times when Freud published his famous texts on the subconscious (*The Interpretation of Dreams* (1899) and *Three Essays on the Theory of Sexuality* (1905), and the famous French philopher Bergson published *Creative Evolution* (L'Evolution créatrice) in 1907. Kandinsky pioneered abstract painting in

Munich in 1911 and contacts were close between the artists of Munich and Paris. It seems Duchamp also read amongst others Nietzsche who was particularly interested also in creativity, Poincaré on the role of the subjective experience and the nominalist Stirner on the uniqueness that can not be described by words because of its very uniqueness. It is also worth mentioning the great influence on Picasso by Poincaré's idea of representing an object in four dimensions by projecting a succession of perspectives (see Arthur L.Miller)

Reflections in glass is the basis for Duchamp's beard and moustache version of Mona Lisa in 1919. A photograph from 1945 shows a shop window that Duchamp arranged in New York and in the photo can be seen both the contents of the windows and the reflection in the glass pane of the profiles of Duchamp as well as that of André Breton.

In the 1920s Duchamp played around with a female alias that he called Rrose Selavy (c'est la vie – meaning eros is life). By eros Duchamps seems to have meant something more like Freud's libido rather than something specifically erotic, however.

55   Ulf Linde: *Marcel Duchamp*. Rabén & Sjögren 1986. Årsbok för statens konstmuseer 32, p 127. Linde mentions the fact that the first *Bicycle Wheel* was made in 1913, two years before the term Ready-made was first used. The first one was made in Neuilly in 1913 and has now disappeared. The second *Bicycle Wheel* (now also disappeared) can be seen in a photograph taken in 1917/18 in Duchamp's studio in New York. The photo is published i.al. in Leah Dickerman: *Introduction* in *Dada* (Catalogue to the 2005 Dada exhibition in Paris, New York and Washington), p 288. In an interview on June 21st, 1967 – just a year before his death - for the French radio l'ORTF, Duchamp, however, mentioned the Bicycle Wheel of 1913 as the first Ready-made, which to

me suggests that he reused the object of 1913 as a Ready-made in 1915 because he thought that for the general public it fitted in with the criteria for a *Ready-made* even though it could hardly be said to do that for himself. Ulf Linde also mentions that The *Bicycle Wheel* might at first have been made more or less as an illustration to Nietzsche's concept of flux (Ur-Ena) where nothing has yet been separated out and to Bergson's *La durée réelle* (1910) and to Duchamp's concept of de-multiplication (only when the wheel stops you can see the spokes).

56   I am here thinking of, for example, his illustration in 1911 to the poem *Encore cet aster* by Laforgue, *Mécanique de la pudeur, Pudeur mécanique.* (1912).

57   Philippe Collin: *Marcel Duchamp parle des ready-made*, p 11. L'Échoppe. Paris 1998.

58   Janine Mileaf and Mattew S. Witkovsky: *Paris* in in *Dada* (Catalogue to the 2005 Dada exhibition in Paris, New York and Washington), p 362.

59   From a speech made by Duchamp in 1957 and published in Art News, vol 56 No 4, Summer 1957 and reprinted as *Marcel Duchamp. Le processus creative* by L'Échoppe 1987.

60   Philippe Collin: *Marcel Duchamp parle des ready-made*, p 10 - 11. L'Échoppe. Paris 1998.

61   Notably in the 1961 catalogue to the exhibition of Kinetic Art at the Moderna Museet in Stockholm 17 May – 3 September 1961.

62   Philippe Collin: *Marcel Duchamp parle des ready-made*, p 11. L'Échoppe. Paris 1998.

In his posthumously published notes he has jotted down the idea of looking for an object on the only basis that it matches a certain weight decided upon in advance. Or even decide on a certain weight for each year and then make sure all Ready-mades of that year are of the same weight. Marcel Duchamp: *Notes* First published by Centre Pompidou 1980. Flammarion 2005, p 107.

63   David Hopkins: *Dada and Surrealism*, p 33. Oxford University Press 2004.

64   Sabine T. Kriebel: *Cologne* in *Dada* (Catalogue to the 2005 Dada exhibition in Paris, New York and Washington), p 222.

65   Janine Mileaf and Mattew S. Witkovsky: *Paris* in in *Dada* (Catalogue to the 2005 Dada exhibition in Paris, New York and Washington), p 350.

66   Leah Dickerman: *Introduction* in *Dada* (Catalogue to the 2005 Dada exhibition in Paris, New York and Washington), p 2.

67   Sabine T. Kriebel: *Cologne* in *Dada* (Catalogue to the 2005 Dada exhibition in Paris, New York and Washington), p 221.

68   According to David Hopkins "Breton was an avid collector of works by psychotic artists such as Joseph Crépin and Hector Hyppolite", and Max Ernst gave a copy of Hans Prinzhorn's book *The Artistery of the Mentally Ill* to Paul Eluard in 1922. David Hopkins: *Dada and Surrealism*. Oxford University Press 2004, p 102.

69   Janine Mileaf and Mattew S. Witkovsky: *Paris* in *Dada* (Catalogue to the 2005 Dada exhibition in Paris, New York and Washington), p 351.

70   Michael R. Taylor: *New York* in *Dada* (Catalogue to the 2005 Dada exhibition in Paris, New York and Washington), p 277 and p 283 for the coming into being in 1920 of a part of Duchamp's *Large Glass*. Hans Arp had used chance for a few collages in 1916-17 (see same catalogue pp 56-57).

71   David Hopkins: *Dada and Surrealism*, p 103. Oxford University Press 2004.

72   Interestingly the Dadaist André Breton claimed in a 1922 lecture that the three movements were "not, on the whole, three distinctive movements;... all three participate in a more general movement, the meaning and breadth of which we still do not precisely know." Quoted in Arnauld Pierre: *The "Confrontation of Modern Values: A Moral History of Dada in Paris*. In Lea Dickerman (Ed.) *The Dada Seminars* p 241. Center for Advanced Study in the Visual Arts. National Gallery of Art, Washington in association with D.A.P.2005.

73   Leah Dickerman (Ed.) in the Introduction to *The Dada Seminars*, p 3. Center for Advanced Study in the Visual Arts. National Gallery of Art, Washington in association with D.A.P.2005.

74   Another example is a piece of art made in 1917 by Augusto Giacometti (a distant relative of Alberto G.), probably overlooked because it seems to have disappeared and there is no other recording of it than the artist's own words. "Yesterday I finished my moving Dadaist work of art. I don't think anyone has created something like this before. My moving piece of art resembles a square cloud with a pendulum of blue smoke" (my translation from the Swedish text in the catalogue to the exhibition of Kinetic Art at the

Moderna Museet in Stockholm 17 May – 3 September 1961, p 4).

75   David Hopkins: *Dada and Surrealism*, p 3-4. Oxford University Press 2004.

76   Arp is quoted by Janine Mileaf and Mattew S. Witkovsky as saying that "the bourgeoisie... has less imagination than a worm". In" *Paris" Dada* (Catalogue to the 2005 Dada exhibition in Paris, New York and Washington), p 359. And Picabia (p 358) writing in the "Festival – Manifeste – Presbyte" in 1920 that "The artist or this bourgeois is but a gigantic unconscious who takes his timidity for honesty!"

77   David Hopkins: *Dada and Surrealism*, p 42. Oxford University Press 2004. C.f. also Duchamp's Houston speech in 1957.

78   Terms used in the 1961 catalogue to the exhibitions of Kinetic Art or Mobile Art in Stockholm and in Holland.

79   Ulf Linde mentions that according to Duchamp he kept the first version in 1913 in his studio for the atmosphere it created, a bit like having a fire going in the fire place. At first it was not intended as a work of art at all. Not even as a *Ready-made*. In 1913 he had not even thought of such a concept. He only did this two years later in New York. Ulf Linde: *Marcel Duchamp*. Rabén & Sjögren 1986. Årsbok för statens konstmuseer 32, p 127.

80   Philippe Collin: *Marcel Duchamp parle des ready-made*, p 14 - 15. L'Échoppe. Paris 1998.

81   Michael R. Taylor: *New York* in *Dada* (Catalogue

to the 2005 Dada exhibition in Paris, New York and Washington), p 283.

82   Hal Foster: *A Bashed Ego: Max Ernst in Cologne.* In Lea Dickerman (Ed.) *The Dada Seminars* pp 129-149. Center for Advanced Study in the Visual Arts. National Gallery of Art, Washington in association with D.A.P.2005.

83   Photographs of a reproduction can be seen in Leah Dickerman: *Dada* (Catalogue to the 2005 Dada exhibition in Paris, New York and Washington), pp 312-313.

84   *Rörelse i Konsten* Catalogue to the exhibition of movement in art 17 May – 3 September 1961.

85   George Baker: *Keep Smiling* in Leah Dickerman (Ed.) *The Dada Seminars* p 211. Center for Advanced Study in the Visual Arts. National Gallery of Art, Washington in association with D.A.P. 2005.

86   Janine Mileaf and Mattew S. Witkovsky: *Paris* in *Dada* (Catalogue to the 2005 Dada exhibition in Paris, New York and Washington), p 361.

87   Krisztina Passuth: *Moholy-Nagy*, p 29. Thames and Hudson 1985.

88   Hal Foster, Rosalind Kraus, Yve-Alain Bois, Benjamin H.D. Buchloh: Art Since 1900, London 2004, p 178

89   Reprinted in *Gabo*. Harvard University Press 1957, p 151-152. Introductory essays by Herbert Read and Leslie Martin.

90   *Rörelse i Konsten* Catalogue to the exhibition of movement in art 17 May – 3 September 1961.

91   Though as so often with Duchamp it is hard to tell. After his visit in Stockholm in September 1968 to assist with the making of a copy of *La Mariée...* for the Moderna Museet in Stockholm, he called Ulf Linde from Copenhagen to suggest that the newly made copy should be photographed somewhere in the deep southern Swedish forest of Småland. That was exactly what one should see through the glass, he said. In Ulf Linde: *Marcel Duchamp*. Rabén & Sjögren 1986. Årsbok för statens konstmuseer 32, p 47.

92   Illustrations in Leah Dickerman: *Dada* (Catalogue to the 2005 Dada exhibition in Paris, New York and Washington), p 74.

93   Two photographs of costumes as well as an explanatory text about Schlemmer and his ballet can be found in Christopher Wilk, ed: *Modernism. Designing a new world.* V&A Publications 2006, pp 126-7.

94   Illustration in Leah Dickerman: *Dada* (Catalogue to the 2005 Dada exhibition in Paris, New York and Washington), p 142.

95   Pedro E. Guerrero: *Calder at Home*, p 149. Archetype Press 1998.

96   Alexander Calder: *Calder. An Autobiography with pictures.* New York 1966, p 113

97   Piet Mondrian:*A New Realism* (1942-43) Reprinted and translated in he collected writings of Mondrian Harry

Holtzman & Martin S. James (Eds): *The New Art – The New Life. The Collected Writings of Piet Mondrian.* 1986 and reprinted 1993.

98   Alexander Calder: *Calder. An Autobiography with pictures.* New York 1966

99   *Alexander Calder 1898 – 1976.* Catalogue to the exhibition at Moderna Museet, Stockholm 1996, pp 53 and 59.

100   Piet Mondrian: *Pure Abstract Art* (1929). The collected writings of Mondrian are to be found in Harry Holtzman & Martin S. James (Eds): *The New Art – The New Life. The Collected Writings of Piet Mondrian.* Thames & Hudson 1986 reprinted 1993 by Da Capo Press, New York.

101   See for example Piet Mondrian: *The New Plastic in Painting* (1917), *Neo-Placticism: The General principle of Plastic Equivalence* (1920) and - in particular - *Jazz and Neo-Plasticism* (1927) that deals not so much with jazz as with open form. The last time he wrote about open form seems to have been in his last essay from 1942-43 *A new Realism.* All reprinted in Harry Holtzman & Martin S. James (Eds): *The New Art – The New Life. The Collected Writings of Piet Mondrian.* Thames & Hudson 1986 reprinted 1993 by Da Capo Press, New York.

102   Pedro E. Guerrero: *Calder at Home,* p 143. Archetype Press 1998.

103   *Alexander Calder.* A video in the series American Masters © 1998 Educational Broadcasting Corporation. ISBN0-7942-0478-3

104   Henry Moore: *Notes on Sculpture* (1937). Reprinted

in *Modern Artists on Art*. Second Ed, p 175. Ed Robert L. Herbert. 2000.

105   Krisztina Passuth: *Moholy-Nagy*. Thames and Hudson 1985, p 215. This piece of art is in the Museum of Modern Art since 1947. Exhibited in the Albers/Moholy-Nagy exhibition at Tate Modern, London, in 2006 but not reproduced in the catalogue!

106   *Rörelse i Konsten* Catalogue to the exhibition of movement in art 17 May – 3 September 1961, my translation.

107   Krisztina Passuth: *Moholy-Nagy*. Thames and Hudson 1985, p 40.

108   Krisztina Passuth: *Moholy-Nagy*. Thames and Hudson 1985, p 20.

109   Krisztina Passuth: *Moholy-Nagy*. Thames and Hudson 1985, p 31.

110   Krisztina Passuth: *Moholy-Nagy*. Thames and Hudson 1985, p 22.

111   Michael White: *Mechano-facture:Dada/Construct-ivism and the Bauhaus*, p 79 in Achim Borchardt-Hume: *Albers and Moholy-Nagy. From the Bauhaus to the New World* Tate Publishing 2006 (catalogue to the exibition).

112   Quote from Rainer K. Wick: *Teaching at the Bauhaus*. Hatje Cantz 2000, p 141.

113   *Der Sturm*. Berlin 1922. No 12. Translated in Krisztina Passuth: *Moholy-Nagy*, p 290 Thames and Hudson 1985.

114   Weitemeier quoted in Rainer K. Wick: *Teaching at the Bauhaus*. Hatje Cantz 2000, p 137.

115   Krisztina Passuth: *Moholy-Nagy*. Thames and Hudson 1985.

116   Krisztina Passuth: *Moholy-Nagy*. Thames and Hudson 1985, p 48.

117   Rainer K. Wick: *Teaching at the Bauhaus*. Hatje Cantz 2000, p 154.

118   Re-published on pp 360-383 in: Krisztina Passuth: *Moholy-Nagy*. Thames and Hudson 1985.

119   Achim Borchardt-Hume, ed: *Albers and Moholy-Nagy. From the Bauhaus to the new world* . Tate Publishing 2006, p 167.

120   Rainer K. Wick: *Teaching at the Bauhaus*. Hatje Cantz 2000, p 141.

121   This letter was printed in the collection of essays by Herbert Read: *The Philosophy of Modern Art* originally published in 1951 and in many reprints later. It was also reprinted in *Gabo*. Harvard University Press 1957, pp 171-173.

122   For a useful discussion of the differences between these two directions of Constructivism as well as further threads leading to Theo van Doesburg's and Max Bill's Concrete Art as well as other connections to Mondrian, Moore, Hepworth and the Surrealists see Hal Foster, Rosalind Kraus, Yve-Alain Bois, Benjamin H.D. Buchloh: Art Since 1900, London 2004, pp 288-289 and pp 470-474.

123   Herbert Read in the Introduction to *Gabo*. Harvard University Press 1957, p 8

124   In the opinion of Charles Saatchi, the man behind Saatchi Gallery at the former County Hall in central London etc, those defining the art market are even fewer. In an interview with the Financial Times Magazine 2007 07 28/29 he said that "The art world is dominated in people's minds by the thousand artists that are very successful, that are handled by the top 50 dealers around the world."... "but the real art world is hundreds of thousands of artists around the world who don't have dealers and are pretty much unrepresented." This drove him to set up http://www.saatchi-gallery.co.uk/ See also Sarah Thornton: *Seven Days in the Art World*. Norton 2008.

125   David Hopkins: *Dada and Surrealism* Oxford University Press 2004, p 146.

126   A term coined by American art critic Lawrence Alloway according to Denise René in Catherine Millet: *Conversations avec Denise René*. Adam Biro, Paris 1991, p 81 and 93.

127   Catherine Millet: *Conversations avec Denise René*. Adam Biro, Paris 1991, p 81.

128   Catherine Millet: *Conversations avec Denise René*. Adam Biro, Paris 1991, p 10-19.

129   Rainer K. Wick: *Teaching at the Bauhaus*. Hatje Cantz 2000, p 137.

130   *Rörelse i Konsten* Catalogue to the exhibition of

movement in art at the Moderna Museet in Stockholm, 17 May – 3 September, 1961.

131   The original essay in Polish from 1931 by Wladyslaw Strzeminski and Katarzyna Kobro was published in French in 1977 as: A. Baudin and P-M. Jedryka: *La composition de l'espace. Les calculs du rythme spatio-temporel,* Lausanne: l'Age d'Homme. 1977. For an initiated comment see Yves-Alain Bois: *Strzeminski and Kobro: In Search of Motivation* (1984), reprinted in *Painting as a Model.* MIT Press 1990.

132   Visually this object looks very much like his paintings *Interférence Oméga* (oil and Plexiglas) 1958-65 and *TUZ-3* (tempera 1966). Reproduced in Werner Spies: *Victor Vasarely.* Thames and Hudson 1971.

133   Henry Moore (1898-1986) *The Sculptor's Aim* (1934). Reprinted in *Modern Artists on Art.* Second Ed, p 173. Ed Robert L. Herbert. 2000.

134   To get an idea of what Johannes Itten stood for see Chapter 5 in Rainer K. Wick: *Teaching at the Bauhaus.* Hatje Cantz, 2000.

135   Frank Popper: *Agam.* New York 1980 (Revised Edition).

136   The expression "Ideomotoric movement" was first used by Pevsner according to Denise René in Catherine Millet: *Conversations avec Denise René.* Adam Biro, Paris 1991, p 81 or maybe, she added, did it first surface in the texts of Bauhaus.

137   One illustration can be found on p 59 in Achim Borchardt-Hume: *Albers and Moholy-Nagy. From the*

Bauhaus to the New World. Tate Publishing 2006 (catalogue to the exibition).

This is described as "Experiments with painting on transparent plastics and with shadows on white background:" in Achim Borchardt-Hume, ed: *Albers and Moholy-Nagy. From the Bauhaus to the New World*. Tate Publishing 2006, p 166.

Robert Morris: *Notes on Sculpture. Part II.* Artforum October 1966.

Edward Lucie-Smith: *Sculpture Since 1945*. Phaidon 1987, p 75.

A photo of this can be found in in Hal Foster, Rosalind Kraus, Yve-Alain Bois, Benjamin H.D. Buchloh: *Art Since 1900*, London 2004, p 555.

Stefan Germer: *Das Jahrhunderding. Ansätze zu einer Theorie und Geschichte des Multiples*, p 35 in Zdenek Felix (ed): *DasJahrhundert des Multiple. Von Duchamp bis zur Gegenwart*. Oktagon Verlag 1994. Catalogue to the exhibition with the same name at Deichtorhallen in Hamburg Sept-October 1994.

Stefan Germer: *Das Jahrhunderding. Ansätze zu einer Theorie und Geschichte des Multiples*, p 31 in Zdenek Felix (ed): *DasJahrhundert des Multiple. Von Duchamp bis zur Gegenwart*. Oktagon Verlag 1994. Catalogue to the exhibition with the same name at Deichtorhallen in Hamburg Sept-October 1994.

Yakoov Agam, Joseph Albers, Bo Ek (alias Pontus Hultén), Pol Bury, Marcel Duchamp, Karl Gerstner, Heinz

Mack, Frank Malina, Man Ray, Enzo Mari, Bruno Munari, Diter Rot, Jesus Raphael Soto, Jean Tingely and Victor Vasarely.

145   Douglas Crimp: *Redefining Site Specificity* in *On the Museum's Ruins*. MIT Press 1993.

146   Stefan Germer: *Das Jahrhunderding. Ansätze zu einer Theorie und Geschichte des Multiples,* p 68 in Zdenek Felix (ed): *Das Jahrhundert des Multiple. Von Duchamp bis zur Gegenwart.* Oktagon Verlag 1994. Catalogue to the exhibition with the same name at Deichtorhallen in Hamburg Sept-October 1994.

147   Catalogue to the exhibition Gustav Metzger Decades: 1959-2009. Serpentine Gallery, London 2009, p 40

148   Catalogue to the exhibition *Gustav Metzger Decades: 1959-2009*. Serpentine Gallery, London 2009, p 48

149   Sophie O'Brien: *Transformation and Transcendence.* In the catalogue to the exhibition *Gustav Metzger Decades: 1959-2009*. Serpentine Gallery, London 2009, p 37.

150   All quotes in this part of the text are taken from Umberto Eco: *The Open Work* Translated by Anna Cancogni and with an introduction by David Robey.   Harvard University Press 1989.

151   Umberto Eco: *The Open Work*. Translated by Anna Cancogni and with an introduction by David Robey. Harvard University Press 1989.) End note on pp 261-262.

152   Guy Brett: *Lygia Clark: in search of the body.* Art

in America, July 1994. Photos of six of the early works by Lygia Clark can be seen in Guy Brett: *Kinetic Art* Studio Vista 1968.

153   *Tid & Plats: Rio de Janeiro 1956-1964*. Exhibition at the Moderna Museet in Stockholm Jan 19 – April 6, 2008. Catalogue with the same name. Curator: Paulo Venancio Filho, professor at Universidade Federal do Rio de Janeiro. Includes photos.

154   Guy Brett: *Lygia Clark: in search of the body*. Art in America, July 1994.

155   Quoted in Guy Brett: *Lygia Clark: in search of the body*. Art in America, July 1994 and on p 61 in Brett: *Kinetic Art*. Studio Vista 1968. Photos of six of the early works by Lygia Clark can also be seen in Hal Foster, Rosalind Kraus, Yve-Alain Bois, Benjamin H.D. Buchloh: Art Since 1900, London 2004, pp 377-378.

156   Suely Rolnik: *The Body's Contagious Memory. Lygia Clark's Return to the Museum*. Brant Publications 1992 (available on the Internet).

157   Vivian Rehberg: *Lygia Clark. Musée des Beaux Arts de Nantes* Frieze Issue 97, March 2006.

158   Guy Brett: *Lygia Clark: in search of the body*. Art in America, July 1994.

159   Suely Rolnik: *The Body's Contagious Memory. Lygia Clark's Return to the Museum*. Brant Publications 1992 (available on the Internet).

160   Guy Brett: *Lygia Clark: in search of the body.* Art in America, July 1994. Photos of six of the early works by Lygia Clark can also be seen in Guy Brett: *Kinetic Art* Studio Vista 1968.

161   Suely Rolnik: *The Body's Contagious Memory. Lygia Clark's Return to the Museum.* Brant Publications 1992 (available on the Internet).

162   Suely Rolnik: *The Body's Contagious Memory. Lygia Clark's Return to the Museum.* Brant Publications 1992 (available on the Internet)

163   Richardo Basbaum quoted in Guy Brett: *The Proposal of Lygia Clark.* An essay published in *Inside the Visible.* The MIT Press 1996.

164   Guy Brett: *The Proposal of Lygia Clark.* An essay published in *Inside the Visible.* MIT Press 1996.

165   *Charlotte Posenenske.* Art International May 1968. Written in February 1968. Full text of this statement can be found in Silvia Eiblmeyr, Astrid Wege, Eva Schmidt: *CharlottePosenenske.* Revolver Books 2005.

166   Documenta 12 Catalogue (2007), p 76. See also p 344 for a short biography and pp 377-378 for list of her works included in the exhibition.

167   Dario Gamboni: *Potential Images. Ambiguity and Indeterminacy in Modern Art.* Reaktion Books 2002.

168   Dario Gamboni: *Potential Images. Ambiguity and Indeterminacy in Modern Art.* Reaktion Books 2002, p 131.

169   See for example Walter Pach 1919 and 1938 quoted in Dario Gamboni: *Potential Images. Ambiguity and Indeterminacy in Modern Art*. Reaktion Books 2002, p 142.

170   Dario Gamboni: *Potential Images. Ambiguity and Indeterminacy in Modern Art*. Reaktion Books 2002, p 77.

171   Dario Gamboni: *Potential Images. Ambiguity and Indeterminacy in Modern Art*. Reaktion Books 2002, p 99. He also quotes (p 136) the poet and critic André Fontainas who in 1916 said about Cubism that it had an "element of enigma or rebus" that he found an advantage "because it gave the brain more to do, and for longer".

172   Joseph Albers quoted in *Rörelse i Konsten*. Catalogue to the exhibition of movement in art at the Moderna Museet in Stockholm, 17 May – 3 September 1961 (My translation).

173   Paul Greenhalgh: *The Modern Ideal*. V&A Publications 2005, p 206. For a more extensive history of this argument see Dario Gamboni's book quoted above. Ernst Gombrich: *Art and Illusion* from 1960 is also of special interest here.

174   Paul Greenhalgh: *The Modern Ideal*. V&A Publications 2005, p 206.

175   Hilary Spurling: *Matisse. The Master*. Hamish Hamilton 2005, p 17.

176   Robert Hughes: *The Shock of the* New. BBC 1980, p 44.

177   For a very interesting analysis of sources of inspiration for Picasso leading up to the making of *Les Demoi-*

selles... see Arthur I. Miller: Les Demoiselles d'Avignon in New Scientist 29/9 2007, p 50. Miller points out the photos of movements by Muybridge, the discovery of X-rays in 1885, primitive Iberian sculpture, Ésprit Jouffret's writings on four dimensional polyhedras, Henri Poincaré's book *Science and Hypothesis* describing the representation of an object by projecting a succession of perspectives and African masks.

178   T.J.Demos. Zurich Dada; *The Aesthetics of Exile.* In *The Dada Seminars,* p 3. Center for Advanced Study in the Visual Arts. National Gallery of Art, Washington in association with D.A.P. 2005.

179   See for example the two lines from T.S Eliot: *Love Song of J.Alfred Prufrock* from 1917: "In the room the women come and go talking of Michelangelo."

180   Sabine T. Kriebel: *Cologne* in *Dada* (Catalogue to the 2005 Dada exhibition in Paris, New York and Washington), p 224 .

181   Ragnar Sandberg, *Dagboksanteckningar1945 – 1972,* p 16. Atlantis 2002.

182   Ragnar Sandberg, *Dagboksanteckningar1945 – 1972,* p 81. Atlantis 2002.

183   Ragnar Sandberg, *Dagboksanteckningar1945 – 1972,* p 190. Atlantis 2002.

184   Ragnar Sandberg, *Dagboksanteckningar1945 – 1972,* p 210. Atlantis 2002.

185   Hilary Spurling. *Matisse. The Master.* Hamish Hamilton 2005, p 330.

186   Hilary Spurling. *Matisse. The Master.* Hamish Hamilton 2005, p 332.

187   Hilary Spurling. *Matisse. The Master.* Hamish Hamilton 2005, p 393.

188   Hilary Spurling. *Matisse. The Master.* Hamish Hamilton 2005, p 418-19.

189   Hilary Spurling. *Matisse. The Master.* Hamish Hamilton 2005, p 360.

190   Hilary Spurling. *Matisse. The Master.* Hamish Hamilton 2005, p 378.

191   Hilary Spurling. *Matisse. The Master.* Hamish Hamilton 2005, p 389.

192   Hilary Spurling. *Matisse. The Master.* Hamish Hamilton 2005, p 380.

193   Victor Vasarely: *Towards the Democratisation of Art.* 1954. Quoted in Anthony Hill: *DATA, Directions in Art, Theory and Aesthetics.* London 1968, p 104.

194   Krisztina Passuth: *Moholy-Nagy.* Thames and Hudson 1985. p 72.

195   Bridget Riley talking to Andrew Graham-Dixon in Robert Kudielka (ed) Bridget Riley: Dialogues on Art. 2003, pp 72-76.

196   See the catalogue to the exhibition of Kinetic Art at the Moderna Museet in Stockholm 17 May – 3 September 1961.

197   Rainer K.Wick: *Teaching at the Bauhaus.* Hatje Cantz 2000, p 136.

198   Dario Gamboni: *Potential Images. Ambiguity and Indeterminacy in Modern Art.* Reaktion Books 2002, p 224 and footnote 39 on p 291.

199   Catherine Millet: *Conversations avec Denise René.* Adam Biro, Paris 1991, p 23.

200   For illustrations as well as factual information about Fahlström see Jean-Francois Chevrier in *Öyvind Fahlström. Another Space for Painting,* Museu d'Art Contemporani de Barcelona 2000 and Sophie Allgårdh (Ed) "*Med världen som spelplan. Öyvind Fahlström*" (with texts also in English). Mjellby Art Museeum, Halmstad, Sweden 2007.

201   Suely Rolnik: *Öyvind Fahlström's Changing Map.* In *Öyvind Fahlström. Another Space for Painting,* p 25. Museu d'Art Contemporani de Barcelona 2000, p 334.

202   Hultberg quoted in Jean-Francois Chevrier in *Öyvind Fahlström. Another Space for Painting,* p 12. Museu d'Art Contemporani de Barcelona 2000.
    Chevrier's long text on Fahlström is a treasure trove for anyone interested in Participatory Art – especially pp 150-153 - and hence it is well worth quoting extensively from it.

203   *4.documenta.* Catalogue 1. Kassel 1968.

204   Nathalie Sarraute's novel *Le Planétarium* was published in 1959 and reprinted as late as in 2003 by Gallimard.

205   See short manuscript by Fahlström quoted in
Öyvind Fahlstöm. Another Space for Painting, p 154. Museu
d'Art Contemporani de Barcelona 2000.

206   *A Game of Character* originally published in Art and
Literature, no 3, 1962 and reprinted in *Öyvind Fahlström.
Another Space for Painting*, p 145-146. Museu d'Art
Contemporani de Barcelona 2000.

207   Jean-Francois Chevrier in *Öyvind Fahlstöm. Another
Space for Painting*, p 25. Museu d'Art Contemporani de
Barcelona 2000.

208   Mike Kelley: *Myth Science* (1995) Reprinted in both
English and a Swedish translation in Sophie Allgårdh (Ed)
"Med världen som spelplan. Öyvind Fahlström" (with texts
also in English). Mjellby Art Museum, Halmstad, Sweden
2007, pp 107 and 153 respectively.

209   Fahlström in *Notes on Ade-Ledic-Nander 2
(1055-1957) and Some Later Developments* quoted in
Öyvind Fahlstöm. Another Space for Painting, Museu d'Art
Contemporani de Barcelona 2000, p 30 note 38.

210   Jean-Francois Chevrier in *Öyvind Fahlstöm.
Another Space for Painting*, Museu d'Art Contemporani de
Barcelona 2000, p 28.

211   Piet Mondrian: *Jazz and the Neo-Plastic* (1927).
Translated and reprinted in Harry Holtzman & Martin
S. James (Eds): *The New Art – The New Life. The Collected
Writings of Piet Mondrian*. 1986 and reprinted 1993.

212   Piet Mondrian: *Painting and Photography* (1927).

Translated and reprinted in Harry Holtzman & Martin S. James (Eds): *The New Art – The New Life. The Collected Writings of Piet Mondrian.* 1986 and reprinted 1993.

213   Cf Leah Dickerman: *Zurich* in *Dada* (Catalogue to the 2005 Dada exhibition in Paris, New York and Washington), p 41. The Swedish writer and painter August Strindberg experimented with this technique, too. His beautiful *Celestography* from 1894 is reproduced in Gamboni, p 175.

214   Brigid Doherty: *Berlin* in *Dada* (Catalogue to the 2005 Dada exhibition in Paris, New York and Washington), pp 90 – 99.

215   Rainer K. Wick: *Teaching at the Bauhaus.* Hatje Cantz 2000, p 136.

216   Krisztina Passuth: *Moholy-Nagy.* Thames and Hudson 1985.

217   Rainer K. Wick: *Teaching at the Bauhaus.* Hatje Cantz 2000, p 135.

218   Rainer K. Wick: *Teaching at the Bauhaus.* Hatje Cantz 2000, p 135.

219   Marianne Stockebrand, ed: *Joseph Albers. Photographien 1928-1955.* Schirmer/Mosel. 1992.

220   Achim Borchardt-Hume in *Two Bauhaus Histories* in Achim Borchardt-Hume:*Albers and Moholy-Nagy. From the Bauhaus to the New World.* Tate Publishing 2006 (catalogue to the exhibition), p 73.

221   Rainer K.Wick: *Teaching at the Bauhaus.* Hatje Cantz 2000, p 136.

222   Michael R.Taylor: *New York* in *Dada* (Catalogue to the 2005 Dada exhibition in Paris, New York and Washington), pp 287-288: "Friends of the artist who visited the studio were treated to a discombobulating installation, where boundaries between the Ready-mades and the surrounding furniture and studio detritus were nonexistent, thus simultaneously challenging their physical surroundings as well as their preconceived notions about art."

223   David Hopkins: *Dada and Surrealism*, p 31-35. Oxford University Press 2004.

224   See photo and text in Christopher Wilk, ed: *Modernism. Designing a new world.* V&A Publications 2006, pp 38-39.

225   Letter to Alfred Barre, 23 november 1936, Archives of Modern Art; cited in Leah Dickerman, *Merz* and Memory, p 111 in Leah Dickerman (Ed.) *The Dada Seminars.* Center for Advanced Study in the Visual Arts. National Gallery of Art, Washington in association with D.A.P.2005. See also Dorothea Dietrich: *Hannover* in *Dada* (Catalogue to the 2005 Dada exhibition in Paris, New York and Washington), pp 176-177.

226   Cited by Leah Dickerman in *Merz and Memory*, p 118. Lea Dickerman (Ed.) *The Dada Seminars.* Center for Advanced Study in the Visual Arts. National Gallery of Art, Washington in association with D.A.P. 2005.

227   Robert Hughes: *The Shock of the New.* BBC, London 1980, p 42.

228   Catherine Millet: *Conversations avec Denise René*. Adam Biro, Paris 1991, p 21.

229   See also Allan Kaprow: *Manifesto*. In *Manifestoes. A Great Bear Pamphlet*. New York: Something Else Press 1966.

230   The following text is based on the richly illustrated *Oiticica in London* published by Tate Modern in conjunction with their Oiticica exhibition in 2007.

231   www.iniva.org

232   Richard Serra in Jane Ure-Smith: *A journey through steel and space*. An interview with Richard Serra. Financial Times June 2/3, 2007.

233   Jane Ure-Smith: *A journey through steel and space*. An interview with Richard Serra. Financial Times June 2/3, 2007.

234   Grasset quoted in Rainer K. Wick: *Teaching at the Bauhaus*. Hatje Cantz 2000, p 94.

235   Rainer K. Wick: *Teaching at the Bauhaus*. Hatje Cantz 2000, p 94.

236   As can be seen, for example, in Margaret Leichner's *Divisions of shapes, sheet from portfolio with notes and coloured plates from the teaching of Paul Klee*. 1928, watercolor over pencil on paper. Now in the Bauhaus Archive. Illustration on p 389 in Jeannine Fiedler (Ed):*Bauhaus*. Köneman 2006 (English edition).

237 Rainer K. Wick: *Teaching at the Bauhaus*. Hatje Cantz 2000, p 101.

238 Rainer K. Wick: *Teaching at the Bauhaus*. Hatje Cantz 2000, p 117.

239 Rainer K. Wick: *Teaching at the Bauhaus*. Hatje Cantz 2000, p 109 According to Wick, Itten was in his methods of analysis of art inspired by Adolf Hölzel (1853 – 1934), his teacher in 1913 at the academy of art in Stuttgart.

240 Rainer K. Wick: *Teaching at the Bauhaus*. Hatje Cantz 2000, p 125-6.

241 A photograph as well as an explanatory text of Dandanah can be seen in Christopher Wilk, ed: *Modernism. Designing a new world.* V&A Publications 2006, pp 58-59. The original is in Deutsches Spielzeugmuseum, Sonneberg.

242 Sol Le Witt: *Paragraphs on Conceptual Art*. Artforum No 10, 1967. The term Conceptual Art seems to have been coined 1961 by Henry Flynt in his essay *Concept Art*. Another Concept Art theoretician as well as artist is Joseph Kosuth. See for example his article "Art after philosophy" in Studio International 1969.

243 Sol Le Witt: *Paragraphs on Conceptual Art*. Artforum No 10, 1967.

244 See for example Nicholas Serota (ed): *Donald Judd*. Tate Publishing 2004 pp 258,260.

245 Sol Le Witt: *Paragraphs on Conceptual Art*. Artforum No 10, 1967.

246 All reproduced in Gilles Néret: *Matisse*. Taschen 2001.

247   Quoted in Hilary Spurling. *Matisse. The Master.* Hamish Hamilton 2005, pp 161-162.

248   Nelck quoted in Hilary Spurling. *Matisse. The Master.* Hamish Hamilton 2005, p 442.

249   Hilary Spurling. *Matisse. The Master.* Hamish Hamilton 2005, p 431.

250   As mentioned earlier, in January 1916, Duchamp wrote from New York to his sister Suzanne (a painter in her own right) in Paris instructing her to choose her own phrase and inscribe it on his ready-made *Bottlerack* as a deliberate art-creating practice.

251   Alain Borer: *The Essential Joseph Beuys.* MIT Press 1997 (Original in German 1997), p 17. Wick (in Rainer K. Wick: *Teaching at the Bauhaus.* Hatje Cantz 2000, p 148) claims that Moholy-Nagy anticipated this statement of Beuys' by almost half a century... In actual fact it seems that this statement goes back all the way to Plato.

252   Alain Borer: *The Essential Joseph Beuys.* MIT Press 1997 (Original in German 1997), p 33.

253   Alain Borer: *The Essential Joseph Beuys.* MIT Press1997 (Original in German 1997), p 26.

254   Alain Borer: *The Essential Joseph Beuys.* MIT Press 1997 (Original in German 1997), p 26.

255   Alain Borer: *The Essential Joseph Beuys.* MIT Press 1997 (Original in German 1997), 27.

256   Mark Rosenthal: *Joseph Beuys: Staging Sculpture.*

Catalogue to the 2005 retrospective exhibition of Beuys at the Tate Modern in London, p 78.

257   Joseph Beuys: *Memorium*, 1986, p 22 as quoted in Mark Rosenthal: *Joseph Beuys: Staging Sculpture*. Catalogue to the 2005 retrospective exhibition of Beuys at the Tate Modern in London, p 109.

258   Alain Borer: *The Essential Joseph Beuys*. MIT Press 1997 (Original in German 1997), p 14.

259   Sean Rainbird: *At the End of the Twentieth Century: Installing After the Act*.
Catalogue to the 2005 retrospective exhibition of Beuys at the Tate Modern in London, p 140.

260   Sean Rainbird: *At the End of the Twentieth Century: Installing After the Act*.
Catalogue to the 2005 retrospective exhibition of Beuys at the Tate Modern in London, p 136.

261   See Adrian Searle: Field for the British Isles. Pamphlet for the Hayward Gallery, London, England (1996) now at http://www.antonygormley.com/viewtext. php?textid=43

262   Anthony Gormley interviewed in "Snittet" a cultural program on Swedish Radio Corporation broadcasted on August 26, 2009

263   Anthony Gormley interviewed in "Snittet" a cultural program on Swedish Radio Corporation broadcasted on August 26, 2009

264   See for example Michael E. Raynor: *The Strategy Paradox*. Currency Doubleday 2007.

265   Scott McNealy: *The advantages of the global village.* Article in the Financial Times June 8, 2005.

266   Paul   Greenhalgh: *The   Modern   Ideal.*   V&A publications 2005, p 248.

267   Nicolas Bourriaud: *L'Art Relationelle* 1998 and the English translation *Relational Aesthetics* 2002. All page numbers in the following refer to the English translation.

268   Nicholas Bourriaud: *L'Art Relationelle* 1998 and the English translation *Relational Aesthetics* 2002, p 14. All page numbers in the following refer to the English translation.

269   Nicholas Bourriaud: *L'Art Relationelle* 1998 and the English translation *Relational Aesthetics* 2002, p 15. All page numbers in the following refer to the English translation.

270   Olafur Eliasson in Engberg-Pedersen & Wind Meyhoff: *At se sig selv sanse. Samtaler med Olafur Eliasson. Samtale* 33. Informations Forlag, p 48.

271   Olafur Eliasson: *Olafur Eliasson.* Phaidon Press 2002, pp 6-33. Quoted in the catalogue of the Olafur Eliasson exhibition at the Astrup Fernley Museeum of Modern Art in Oslo 2004, p 90.

272   Olaf Eliasson, too, has been influenced by reading the French philosopher Bergson. See Olafur Eliasson in Engberg-Pedersen & Wind Meyhoff: *At se sig selv sanse. Samtaler med Olafur Eliasson. Samtale* 33. Informations Forlag. 2004. p 153.

273   Olafur Eliasson in Engberg-Pedersen & Wind

Meyhoff: *At se sig selv sanse. Samtaler med Olafur Eliasson. Samtale* 33. Informations Forlag. 2004. p 54.

274   Financial Times *A kingdom of the unexpected* July 13, 2007 p 11.

275   Documenta 12 catalogue 2007, pp 220-221, 333 and 359.

276   Documenta 12 catalogue 2007, pp 234-235, 335 and 363.

277   For further discussion of the classical art market, see Fahlström's manifesto: Take Care of the World, in *Öyvind Fahlstöm. Another Space for Painting*, p 154. Museu d'Art Contemporani de Barcelona 2000. And also, in the same book, in the essay by Suely Rolnik p 336

278   Stefan Germer: *Das Jahrhundertding. Ansätze zu einer Theorie und Geschichte des Multiples, p 37* in Zdenek Felix (Ed): *Das Jahrhundert des MULTIPLE. Von Duchamp bis zur Gegenwart.* Okton Verlag 1994. Catalogue to the exhibition of Multiple Art in Deichtorhallen, Hamburg, Sept-Oktober 1994.

279   As quoted by Jean-Francois Chevrier in *Öyvind Fahlstöm. Another Space for Painting*, p 10. Museu d'Art Contemporani de Barcelona 2000.

280   David Hopkins: *Dada and Surrealism.* Oxford University Press 2004, p 80.

281   James P. Womack, Daniel T. Jones & Daniel Roos:

The Machine That Changed the World. Simon & Schuster 2007 edition, p VII.

282   See for eg. James Womak, Daniel T. Jones & Daniel Roos: *The Machine That Changed the World.* (1990) Simon & Shuster 2007.

283   Fahlström in Jean-Francois Chevrier in *Öyvind Fahlström. Another Space for Painting,* p 150. Museu d'Art Contemporani de Barcelona 2000.

284   Chevrier in *Öyvind Fahlström. Another Space for Painting,* p 9-10. Museu d'Art Contemporani de Barcelona 2000.

285   Chevrier in *Öyvind Fahlström. Another Space for Painting,* p 150. Museu d'Art Contemporani de Barcelona 2000.

286   Quoted in *Öyvind Fahlström. Another Space for Painting,* p 16. Museu d'Art Contemporani de Barcelona 2000.

287   Quoted in *Öyvind Fahlström. Another Space for Painting,* p 19. Museu d'Art Contemporani de Barcelona 2000.

288   D.W. Winnicott *Playing and Reality* Routledge 1971, p 86.

289   D.W. Winnicott *Playing and Reality* Routledge 1971, p 73.

290   Jean-Francois Chevrier in *Öyvind Fahlström. Another Space for Painting*, p 20. Museu d'Art Contemporani de Barcelona 2000.

291   Jean-Francois Chevrier quoting Umberto Eco in *Öyvind Fahlström. Another Space for Painting*, Note 30, p 30. Museu d'Art Contemporani de Barcelona 2000. (The French translation *L'oevre ouverte* was published by 'Editions de Seuil in 1965).

292   Jean-Francois Chevrier quoting Umberto Eco in *Öyvind Fahlström. Another Space for Painting*, Note 30, p 30. Museu d'Art Contemporani de Barcelona 2000.

293   Piet Mondrian *Plastic Art and Pure Plastic Art* (1937). Reprinted in *Modern Artists on Art*. Second Ed 2000. Ed Robert L. Herbert, p 152.

294   Piet Mondrian: *Plastic Art and Pure Plastic Art* (1937). Reprinted in *Modern Artists on Art*. Second Ed 2000. Ed. Robert L. Herbert, pp 161-162.

295   Piet Mondrian: *Plastic Art and Pure Plastic Art* (1937). Reprinted in *Modern Artists on Art*. Second Ed 2000. Ed. Robert L. Herbert, p 159.

296   Piet Mondrian: *Plastic Art and Pure Plastic Art* (1937). Reprinted in *Modern Artists on Art*. Second Ed 2000. Ed. Robert L. Herbert, pp 163-164.

297   Piet Mondrian: *Plastic Art and Pure Plastic Art* (1937). Reprinted in *Modern Artists on Art*. Second Ed 2000. Ed. Robert L. Herbert, p 159

298   Piet Mondrian: *Plastic Art and Pure Plastic Art*

(1937). Reprinted in *Modern Artists on Art.* Second Ed 2000. Ed. Robert L. Herbert, p 161

299   Norbert M. Schmitz: *Teaching by Wassily Kandinsky and Paul Klee* in Jeannine Fiedler (Ed):*Bauhaus.* Köneman 2006 (English edition), pp 382 – 391.

300   Arthur C. Danto: *The abuse of beauty.* Daedalus, Fall 2002.

301   See for example my Plexiglas rectangles from 1982, or granite spheres from 1993.